Inner Child Healing and Hypnosis

A practical guide for hypnotherapists

Jackie Thomson

Copyright © 2025 Jackie Thomson

All rights reserved.

ISBN: 978-1-9191715-0-0

Dedication

To those doing the work – on both sides of the chair

Contents

	Foreword	i
	Acknowledgements	v
	Introduction	vii
1	Why Inner Child Healing Matters	1
2	The Hypnotherapist's Role	7
3	Understanding the Inner Child	13
4	Inner Child Archetypes & Wounds	25
5	Client Assessment & Readiness	33
6	Creating a Safe Therapeutic Space	41
7	Navigating & Framing Resistance	51
8	Louise Hay and the Inner Child	57
9	Core Techniques for Inner Child Healing	67
10	Advanced Techniques for Deeper Healing	77
11	Creating a Multi-Session Framework	85
12	Measuring Progress & Deepening the Work	95
13	The Therapist's Inner Work	103
14	Bringing it All Together	113
	Reclaiming the Lost Parts	117
	Resources and Further Reading	119
	About the Author	121
	Index	123

Foreword

Some books teach us something new.

Others make us feel seen.

Jackie Thomson's *Inner Child Healing & Hypnosis* somehow manages to do both - and then some!

When I first heard Jackie was writing this, I had a good feeling about it.

Jackie is someone I've always liked and respected, not just for her skill as a hypnotherapist, but for the quiet integrity she brings to everything she does.

She doesn't make noise for the sake of it.

She listens deeply, speaks when it matters, and knows how to hold space in a way that feels safe, steady, and real.

That's what you'll find in these pages.

This isn't a book full of gimmicks or over-promises.

It's thoughtful.

Grounded. Deep.

And, above all, honest.

Inner child work is having a bit of a moment, isn't it? But the way Jackie approaches it...it's not about trends. It's about truth. About the stories our clients carry that were written long before they had words. About the parts of ourselves we learned to hide - or forget altogether - just to get through.

And I say that not as someone who just "knows the theory." I say that as someone who's lived it.

I was adopted at six weeks old. A loving home, yes. Supportive family, absolutely.

But for a long time, there was a quiet question living in my body that I couldn't quite name. Something about not feeling fully chosen. Or maybe not quite real. I didn't even recognise it as a wound at first - just this background hum of needing to prove I was worth keeping.

It wasn't until I started exploring my own inner child that this came to the surface. Not as a big dramatic event, but as a softness, a sadness, that needed witnessing.

There was another moment that stays with me, too. I was five. My teacher was handing out gold stars. I'd done everything right - tidy handwriting, quiet, helpful.

She passed me by. No star. Just moved on.

I know it sounds small, but in that moment, something in me shifted. I told myself: *You must not be enough.*

That belief stayed with me for years.

It showed up in perfectionism, overworking, that need to always "get it right."

All because a five-year-old didn't get a sticker.

Foreword

That's the thing about childhood wounds. They don't always shout. Sometimes, they whisper. But they shape us all the same.

This is why Jackie's work is so important. She doesn't just help us understand these wounds - she helps us approach them with care.

She's written a book that's as practical as it is profound.

It has structure, yes - techniques, models, session frameworks - but it also has soul. It reminds us that before we're therapists, we're human. And that healing isn't about fixing people, it's about reconnecting them to the parts they've had to silence to survive.

For anyone new to inner child work, this book is a beautiful place to start.

For those of us who've been working this way for a while, it's a chance to reconnect to the heart of the process - and maybe even find something new in ourselves along the way.

What I admire most is how Jackie encourages us to do the work ourselves. To pause. To reflect. To meet our own inner child with the same patience we offer to others. That's brave. And it's necessary. Because we can only walk with clients as far as we're willing to go ourselves.

This book doesn't rush. It invites. It doesn't preach. It shares. And it doesn't promise quick fixes - because this work isn't about speed. It's about depth.

Jackie, thank you.

For your honesty, your care and your clarity.

This is the kind of book that doesn't just sit on a shelf. It sits with you. It lingers. It works on you, quietly, in the best possible way.

If you're holding this book now, I hope you let it in. Let it guide you - not just as a practitioner, but as a person. Because healing the inner child isn't just something we offer our clients. It's something we all need.

And, thanks to Jackie, we have one of the most thoughtful and compassionate guides to walk us through it.

Sheila Granger
Hypnotherapist, Author & Trainer
July 2025

Acknowledgments

I wouldn't be where I am today without the love and support of my husband, Mark, and my family. You've walked with me through every chapter of this journey, and there have been plenty of moments when I've truly needed you. Thank you.

To the trainers and mentors who have helped shape my path in hypnotherapy - Dr Kate Beaven-Marks, Rory Fulcher, Sheila Granger, Turan Mirza, Linda Witchell - thank you for your guidance, generosity and belief in me.

I'm eternally grateful to my Heal Your Life® trainers, Dr Patricia Crane and Eileen Clair, and to my mentors and friends Jane Matthews, Lynn Meadowcroft and Rick Nichols. Your presence and guidance helped make my own healing possible.

Thank you also to those who generously gave their time to read the manuscript and share thoughtful feedback. Your insights helped make this a better book.

Each of you has helped shape this work in ways you may never fully realise.

"Sometimes our light goes out, but is blown again into flame by an encounter with another human being. Each of us owes the deepest thanks to those who have rekindled this inner light."
Albert Schweitzer

Introduction

If you had told me twenty years ago that I would end up writing a book on inner child healing and hypnosis for other hypnotherapists, I probably would have laughed. Not because I didn't believe in personal transformation but because, back then, I hadn't even begun to understand the depth of my own wounds, let alone how they were affecting every area of my life.

This book was born out of experience - my own and that of the many clients and students I've had the privilege to work with. I discovered inner child healing after a life event that brought me to my knees and forced me to rebuild from the inside out.

It all began with a message on my computer screen which confirmed something I'd feared but tried to ignore: my husband was having an affair. That moment shattered everything I thought I knew. It forced me to walk away from the business I'd built and then shared with him, the life I thought I'd live and the familiar comforts that had defined me for decades.

What followed was a long, often painful, journey of rediscovery - a journey that eventually led me to the concept of the inner child. I first came across this idea through Louise Hay's Heal Your Life work, and it blew me away. It helped me make sense of why I'd tolerated certain behaviours, why I doubted myself so deeply, and why I often felt as if something inside me was silently crying out for comfort.

What started as personal growth soon became a powerful element of my professional practice, especially when I trained in hypnotherapy and began to see just how much unspoken pain people carry from their early years. It felt natural to integrate what I'd learned into my practice.

Again and again, I saw how my clients were carrying their own wounded inner children. Children who had felt abandoned, dismissed, criticised, unheard or simply not enough. These clients weren't 'broken', they were simply doing their best to cope with wounds that had never been given the chance to heal.

So, this book is for you if you're a hypnotherapist who:

- wants to work more deeply with clients who present with anxiety, low self-worth, relationship issues, or patterns of self-sabotage

- senses there's more going on beneath the surface than clients initially reveal

- wants to guide clients safely and compassionately through healing their inner child

This process isn't about regressing clients to relive

Introduction

trauma. It's about creating a safe space for the subconscious to bring forward what's ready to be seen, understood and healed. It's about helping people reconnect with the parts of themselves they silenced, perhaps sometimes had to silence, in order to survive.

Inner child work isn't a 'quick fix.' It's layered, nuanced, and often surprising. But it's also one of the most powerful tools I've encountered in supporting lasting emotional change. If you're ready to bring this work into your practice or deepen what you already do, this book will give you the understanding, structure and a few simple approaches to get started.

Each chapter in this book begins with a quote; something to pause with, reflect on, or carry into the work that follows. At the end of each chapter, you'll find my thoughts, a moment to gather what's been explored before we move on. I invite you to take your time with both. Sometimes, the quietest lines are the ones that stay with us longest.

And because I know that sometimes we need more than just what fits between the covers of a book, I've created a free companion guide available for download. With scripts, affirmations, metaphors and journalling prompts, it's designed to support both your client practice and your own ongoing development.

You can download it at:
www.jackiethomson.com/icguide

You don't need to be a trauma expert to begin this work. But you do need to show up with presence, patience and respect for the younger parts of your clients who may finally be ready to speak.

If you're ready to guide your clients toward a better relationship with themselves, so they can live happier, more fulfilled lives, then you're in the right place. You may even find it brings something valuable to your own life too.

How to use this book

This book is designed to offer you a flexible, client-centred approach to bringing inner child healing into your hypnotherapy practice. It's not a rigid protocol or step-by-step manual, but a guide you can adapt to your own style and, most importantly, to the needs of the client in front of you.

Some chapters focus on structure and theory, offering background, frameworks and key concepts. Others suggest practical techniques or reflective elements you can draw from and shape. You're invited to pick up what resonates, adapt what needs adapting and leave the rest.

Because the approaches mentioned here are built on emotional exploration and subconscious healing, they may not align with all therapeutic models. For example, if you are trained in solution-focused therapy, some techniques may feel outside your usual repertoire, and that's okay. This book is best suited to those who feel drawn to working at depth with clients experiencing issues such as low self-worth, anxiety or relational patterns linked to early life experience.

Every client, and every practitioner, experiences the

world differently. Some will visualise easily while others may connect more through physical sensation, memory, metaphor or emotion. You may also encounter clients who are neurodivergent - such as those are who autistic, ADHD or aphantasic - who experience the world in different ways. These approaches can be adapted to suit different ways of processing and expressing, and I encourage you to explore what works best in your own practice.

A note on the illustrations

The illustrations throughout this book are designed to symbolise emotional states, inner experiences, and therapeutic themes. They are not intended to represent specific identities, cultures, or physical characteristics. As hypnotherapists, it's important to be mindful of the diverse backgrounds, beliefs, and experiences our clients bring to the therapy room. Inner child work is as unique as each client and the issues they present with.

So, let's begin.

Chapter 1
Why Inner Child Healing Matters

"There is no salvation in becoming adapted to a world which is crazy."

Henry Miller

We are shaped by our earliest experiences, often far more than we realise, because childhood doesn't stay in childhood. It echoes forward into every corner of adult life, sometimes loudly, sometimes quietly, but always persistently. For many clients, the pain they carry today isn't about what's happening now. It's about wounds left unacknowledged, unmet needs, and coping mechanisms that were once protective but now hold them back.

In the therapy room, clients come in talking about anxiety, addiction, self-sabotage, depression, or relationship breakdowns. But when we look beneath the surface, we often find the same root: a wounded inner child still carrying unmet needs, unprocessed pain, or distorted beliefs formed long ago.

We often think of trauma in terms of extreme events and, yes, those are part of the picture. But inner child healing shows us that trauma can also be silent. It can be the loneliness of a child sent away to boarding school who learns to suppress all emotion to survive. It can be the subtle withdrawal of a parent who was physically present but emotionally absent. It can be a smile that covered up shame or a laugh that hid fear.

Some wounds are more visible. A boy who was beaten daily by his father grows up with rage, fear or addiction as his constant companions. A girl whose boundaries were violated may learn to disconnect from her body, or seek validation through sex or control. A child who grows up watching a toxic relationship unfold may find themselves repeating it, even as they promise never to do so. Or the child sent away to school, aching with loneliness and confusion, might become the adult who seeks connection in the shadows of pornography or sex addiction - longing for closeness but terrified of real vulnerability.

And then there are the 'good' children - high achievers, carers, peacekeepers. The ones who learned early on that love must be earned, that emotions are inconvenient, or that their worth depends on how well they serve others. These same children often grow into adults plagued by anxiety, perfectionism, burnout, or a deep and nameless sadness.

These patterns don't emerge randomly. They are echoes - survival strategies carried from childhood into adulthood. And because many of them are subconscious, the adult has no idea where the behaviour is coming from.

"Why do I keep doing this?" they ask. "Why do I feel like this?" The answer often lies with a younger version of themselves still holding the wound.

Inner child healing isn't about blame. It's about understanding. It's about recognising how the past shows up in the present, and giving clients the tools to create a new future. One where they're not just surviving but truly living.

A moment from my journey

When I first moved to a new town after the breakdown of my marriage, I was starting over in every sense. I had left behind everything familiar; friends, routines, even the usual streets I'd drive down. I had a roof over my head and a business I could still run remotely, but I felt utterly alone.

For the first few weeks, I hardly left the house except for essentials. The staff at the local shops were the only people I spoke to. I remember sitting one evening in the quiet, realising just how heavy the loneliness felt. I didn't cry - not then - but underneath it all, that was a sadness I hadn't quite faced yet. I wasn't ready.

At the time, I didn't have the language for what I was feeling. I didn't know about the inner child, or how old emotions can echo through new experiences. But I knew something inside me felt forgotten. I didn't feel like me. I was just someone trying to get through the day.

It was only much later that I began learning about inner child work, and then I recognised what had really been happening. That sadness wasn't just about being in a new place, it was the voice of a younger part of me who had felt small, lost or left behind long before I ever packed up the car.

Looking back, that chapter of my life showed me something important: that our current struggles often carry the whispers of old wounds. And that healing doesn't always start with knowing, sometimes it starts with noticing.

So, inner child healing matters because it is at the root of so much suffering. Because it explains what often seems inexplicable. Because it gives clients the tools to stop repeating the past. And because every healed child within an adult creates a ripple of change - not just for them, but for those around them and the generations to come.

As hypnotherapists, we are uniquely placed to guide this work. The subconscious remembers everything. It holds the maps of our early emotional landscape, the imprints of unmet needs and the echoes of long-lost joy. With hypnosis, we can guide clients to connect with, comfort, and re-integrate these lost parts of themselves - not to relive trauma but to meet it with compassion and care.

A thought from me

Looking back, I can see that the loneliness I felt in that new town wasn't just about the present, it was something older surfacing.

At the time, I didn't know about the inner child. I just knew something didn't feel right. And sometimes, that's where healing begins; not with answers but with noticing what wants to be felt.

We don't need to understand everything before we begin. We just need to be open to listening - to our clients and to ourselves.

In the next chapter, we'll explore the hypnotherapist's role in this.

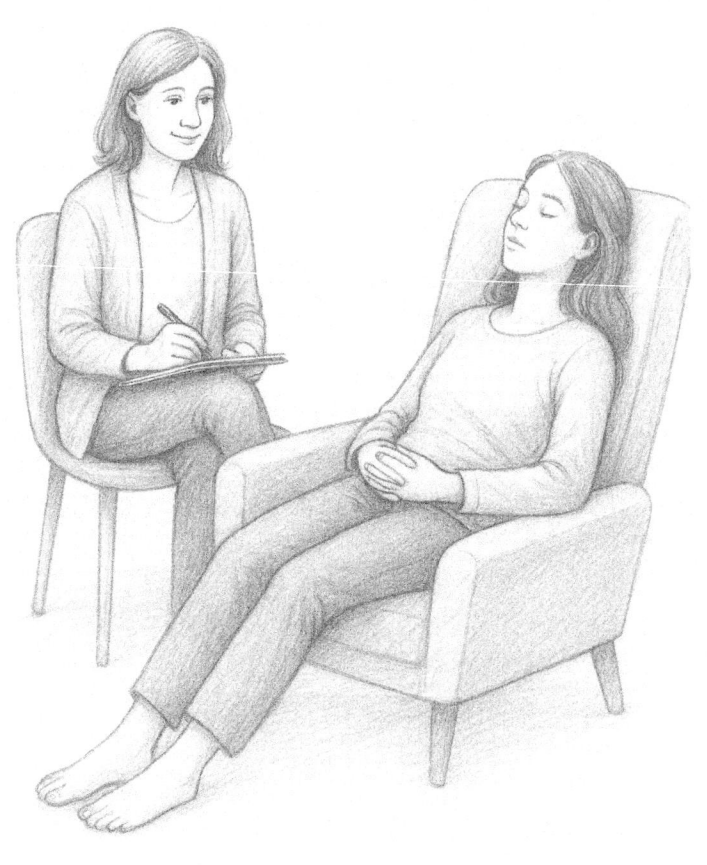

Chapter 2
The Hypnotherapist's Role

"I believe that this neglected, wounded, inner child of the past is the major source of human misery."

John Bradshaw

Bringing inner child healing into hypnotherapy requires more than just knowing the best techniques, scripts or visualisations. It asks us to hold space in a way that is deeply compassionate, trauma-aware and grounded in trust. As hypnotherapists, we become both guides and witnesses, facilitating a process that can be emotional and raw yet profoundly healing.

Being a Compassionate Witness

Clients may well share things they've never voiced before - not because they've been hiding them deliberately, but because they've been buried deep within the subconscious. When we work with the inner child, we're often helping clients access memories or feelings that were too big, too painful or too confusing for them to process at the time. Our role is to hold space without judgement, and without rushing to fix.

Sometimes, all a client's inner child needs is to be seen and heard.

We can do this by:

- validating the client's emotional experience, even if we can't logically 'make sense' of it
- allowing silence and emotion to unfold without interruption
- reassuring the adult client that it's safe to feel what's coming up.

This kind of presence is healing in itself. Many clients have never had someone sit with them like that before.

A moment from my journey

I remember working with a client who seemed very together on the surface. She was successful, articulate, and emotionally 'in control.' But when we began some inner child work, something shifted. She paused mid-sentence, her eyes welled up, and she whispered, "I didn't think this would feel so real."

My instinct was to reach in, to soothe, to offer words. But something in me said: just stay. Just be with her. So I did. We sat together in silence, and she cried. No drama, no breakthrough, just a quiet moment of being witnessed. Afterwards, she said, "I've never had anyone just sit with me like that."

I've come to understand that this is where the real work often happens; not in the techniques or scripts, but in our presence. And if I hadn't done my own healing work, I don't think I would have been able to sit with that silence. I might have rushed to reassure, changed the subject, or filled the space with words.

Instead, I let her feel what needed to be felt, and trusted that that would be enough.

Trauma Sensitivity and Ethical Awareness

Inner child work is not appropriate for every client, or at every stage of their journey. Clients with active trauma symptoms, particularly those with complex PTSD or dissociative symptoms, may need stabilisation and specialist support before engaging in regression or deep emotional processing.

Ask yourself, does this client have emotional resilience and support in place? Are they able to stay grounded and self-regulate when difficult emotions arise? Have I clearly explained what inner child work involves, including the potential for emotional intensity?

Informed consent, ongoing dialogue and the ability to pause or adapt the work are essential. Clients must always feel they are in control of the process.

If you are not trained to work with complex trauma, addiction or severe mental health presentations, it is important to refer on or seek supervision before engaging in deep inner child work with these clients. This approach can be incredibly powerful, but also requires us to know our limits and work within our training. This isn't a limitation, but a sign of professionalism. Knowing when to stay within your scope and when to reach out for support is part of ethical, effective practice, which ensures safer and more effective outcomes for everyone.

Your Own Inner Work Matters

We can only take clients as deep as we've been willing to go ourselves. If you've never explored your own inner child, I wholeheartedly encourage you to do so; either through self-reflection, journalling, creative expression or receiving therapy or hypnosis yourself. Not only will this deepen your understanding, it will help you avoid projecting, rescuing or over-identifying with your clients.

Clients are intuitive. They can feel when we're coming from a place of wholeness and calm versus when we're triggered ourselves. Doing our own inner work helps us:

- stay grounded and neutral in sessions
- maintain better boundaries
- trust the client's pace without rushing the emotional process

Inner child healing opens the door to a space that's deeply human - tender, vulnerable and meaningful. What makes this work so powerful isn't just the techniques you use but the way you show up: with kindness, patience and a genuine willingness to accept your clients exactly as they are without judgement.

A thought from me

The inner child is the part of us that still remembers not just what happened, but how it felt. Healing begins when we're willing to listen.

Each time we sit with a client's pain without rushing to fix it, we offer something powerful – presence. And in doing so, we honour not only their healing but our own capacity to hold space with compassion and care.

In the next chapter, we'll explore what the inner child really is and how to begin understanding its place in the therapeutic journey.

Chapter 3
Understanding The Inner Child

"Knowing your own darkness is the best method for dealing with the darknesses of other people."

Carl Jung

Before we can support our clients through inner child healing, we need to understand what or who the inner child is, and what this work is really about. It isn't about nostalgia or looking back for the sake of it. It's about recognising how unprocessed emotions from childhood can quietly shape adult lives in powerful, often unconscious ways.

My definition of the inner child: "A part of the subconscious mind, a vital part of the psyche, which holds childhood memories, experiences, and emotions.

It's the part that holds the key to our deepest emotions, needs and dreams. It is the source of our creativity, joy and spontaneity, but also of our pain, fear and insecurity."

A moment from my journey

Before I fully understood the idea of the inner child, I had my own experience of what it felt like to carry those early emotions into adulthood.

Looking back, I can see how often I was running on autopilot; high-functioning on the outside but carrying layers of emotion I didn't know how to name. I'd built a life around being capable, helpful and dependable. And I was. But I now realise how much of that was driven by a younger part of me still trying to earn love and approval.

It wasn't until I began exploring this idea of the inner child (not as a concept but as a real, feeling part of myself) that things started to change. I remember sitting with a journal, unsure what to write, and then suddenly the words tumbled out. Not in adult language but in the voice of a little girl who felt lost, scared, and tired of trying so hard to be good.

That moment changed everything. I knew then I wasn't broken. I was carrying an emotional blueprint that had never been updated. And in recognising her voice, I could begin to listen differently. Not just to myself but to the clients who came through my door, carrying the echoes of their own childhood pain too.

When a child is nurtured by loving parents, is allowed to express their feelings and guided to appropriate action and expression for those feelings, they're likely to grow up emotionally balanced, able to accept and take healthy action on their feelings.

When a child grows up in a dysfunctional environment - one lacking in nurture and possibly affected by negative patterns passed down through generations - feelings and emotions may be repressed. In such environments, where shaming, belittling, invalidation, discouragement, and even physical, emotional, or sexual abuse are present, the child may unconsciously adopt a specific 'role' within the family. This role serves as a coping mechanism, helping the child to survive and adapt to the challenging circumstances.

So, at an unconscious level, the child may become a caretaker or parent child, a sickly child, a perfect child, a rebel child, a bad child or an over-achiever. And these roles stay with them into adulthood, resulting in issues such as anger or temper tantrums, promiscuity, addictive behaviour, relationship issues and illness. And they can become deeply ingrained, long after they're no longer needed.

Various therapeutic models have touched on the idea of the inner child, sometimes directly, sometimes in more symbolic terms. Here are some examples:

Carl Jung and the Child Archetype

The idea of the inner child isn't new. The concept of archetypes was introduced by Carl Jung, one of the founding voices in modern psychology, who suggested that archetypes are patterns or symbolic images that arise from the collective unconscious - a concept from Jungian psychology which suggests we all share a deep, inherited layer of the mind. These archetypes also reflect our shared human experience, shaping how we see ourselves and the world around us. Among them was the Child Archetype, which he believed represented both our childhood innocence and our capacity for growth and transformation; the part of us that is full of possibility, wonder, and creativity, but also the part that feels most vulnerable and in need of care.

Jung believed this archetype appears in dreams, myths and spiritual traditions as concepts such as the 'divine child', the 'wounded child' or the 'magical child', carrying powerful messages about our emotional life and how these aspects might manifest in childhood. He suggested these inner patterns weren't just ideas, but real parts of the psyche that could influence how we think, feel and relate to the world around us.

When we connect with the child archetype in therapeutic work, we're tapping into the source of our earliest emotional blueprint. Sometimes it will surface as longing or fear, and sometimes as the creative spark we've suppressed over time. Inner child healing allows us to help clients reconnect with what's been lost or wounded and, in doing so, unlock hidden potential for acceptance, healing and understanding.

Transactional Analysis and the Child Ego State

Eric Berne's Transactional Analysis (TA) offers a simple yet powerful model for understanding human behaviour. At its core are three ego states: Parent, Adult, and Child. These are not roles, but psychological states we move in and out of.

The Child Ego State is further divided into:

- **The Natural Child**: spontaneous, joyful, curious
- **The Adapted Child**: compliant or rebellious, shaped by external expectations and early conditioning
- **The Little Professor**: creative problem-solver, intuitive and imaginative.

The Child ego state holds our earliest emotional memories, along with our spontaneity, vulnerability and need for love. When a client responds with emotional intensity, fear or defensiveness that seems disproportionate to the situation, it's often this ego state being activated.

Inner child work aligns beautifully with TA. Hypnosis can help clients access the adapted or natural child states, reconnecting them with their original spontaneity and helping to soothe the parts of them that adapted to survive.

Schema Therapy

Developed by Jeffrey Young, Schema Therapy brings together ideas from cognitive behavioural therapy (CBT), attachment theory and Gestalt therapy. It focuses on identifying and changing ingrained, often negative patterns of thinking, feeling and behaving - emotional patterns known as schemas – which often begin in childhood when core emotional needs aren't met.

Schemas are deeply held beliefs or assumptions we make about ourselves and the world, often formed through early experience. They tend to sit just beneath the surface but can influence everything from self-worth to relationships and decision-making.

Some common examples include:

- **Abandonment** – *"People will leave me."*
- **Defectiveness/Shame** – *"There's something wrong with me."*
- **Emotional Deprivation** – *"My needs will never be met."*
- **Subjugation** – *"I must put others first and keep quiet about my own needs."*

These patterns often follow clients into adulthood, quietly shaping how they see themselves and how they relate to others, until something invites them to look more closely.

Inner child work addresses the emotional roots of these schemas. Whilst cognitive work challenges the belief, hypnosis and inner child healing go deeper, offering clients the experience of their unmet needs being seen, heard, and honoured, often for the first time.

Inner Bonding, Parts Therapy, and Other Modalities

Many modern therapeutic approaches build on the idea that we're made up of different inner parts. Each part has its own voice, its own fear, its own unmet needs. Inner child healing sits comfortably within this framework.

- **Inner Bonding**, developed by Margaret Paul, uses a six-step process to help clients build a connection between their wounded inner child and a wise, loving adult self. Through inner dialogue and compassionate attention, clients begin to meet their emotional needs from within, rather than looking for external approval or rescue.

- **Parts Therapy**, inspired by Charles Tebbetts and further developed by Roy Hunter, uses hypnosis to open communication between different aspects of the subconscious. A protective part might be doing its best to keep someone safe, even if that means keeping the inner child hidden or silent. Hypnosis allows these parts to be heard without judgement, understood and realigned.

- **Gestalt Therapy**, pioneered by Fritz Perls, offers tools like the 'empty chair' technique, where clients can give voice to different parts of themselves, including the inner child, by speaking to them as if they were present. This process can be helpful when clients struggle to name what they feel or need. Giving a voice to different parts of themselves often unlocks emotion and insight that's been suppressed or held back.

- Other approaches, such as **Internal Family Systems** and **Voice Dialogue**, also explore the idea of inner parts or subpersonalities. These models are valuable when clients carry strong protective patterns, or when deeper emotional responses feel unreachable. They affirm something very important - that we're not broken. We're simply carrying protective strategies and vulnerable parts that have not yet been acknowledged. Exploring these inner parts helps them feel seen, without overwhelm.

These models enrich the inner child healing process, offering structure, language and safety for working with the often-fragile emotions held within.

In practice, we see the inner child show up in everyday adult behaviours:

- The client who's desperate to please and terrified of rejection.
- The person who lashes out when they feel unseen, even if they can't explain why.
- The overachiever who never feels good enough, no matter their success.

What's key is recognising that these responses aren't irrational or dramatic. They're protective.

These coping strategies were learned early on, often in childhood, as ways to manage pain, fear, or unmet emotional needs. They helped the child feel safe, or at least safer. But what once worked for survival can become much more of a barrier in adult life, making it harder to connect with others, regulate emotions or experience joy.

Hypnotherapy offers a unique way to reach those younger parts of the subconscious with care and curiosity. Through regression, visualisation and safe inner dialogue, we can guide clients to reconnect with the child within - not to relive the past, but to bring understanding, validation and healing that may never have been available to them at the time.

This process can help clients begin to recognise and soothe their emotional triggers, rather than being overwhelmed by them. It encourages the development of a more balanced and compassionate inner dialogue; one that replaces self-criticism with understanding. Clients often begin to rediscover parts of themselves that were pushed aside to survive - their creativity, their confidence, their sense of play. And over time, this work can support real, lasting change, helping to shift emotional patterns that talking alone may not fully reach.

Understanding the inner child means recognising that every adult carries echoes of who they were as a child. And often, those echoes are calling not for analysis, but for healing.

A thought from me

Every part of us has a reason for being, even the ones that confuse, frustrate or embarrass us. The overachiever, the people-pleaser, the perfectionist, the angry child, they all came into being for a reason. They helped us feel safe, loved, or accepted in a world that didn't always feel that way. These parts may seem disruptive now but they were once protectors, doing the best they could with what they knew.

When we stop trying to silence or fix them, and instead turn toward them with understanding and compassion, something begins to shift. We realise we don't need to reject or remove those parts; we just need to listen to them. Healing doesn't come from judgement. It comes from relationship. Relationship with ourselves, with our past and with the younger parts of us that are still waiting to be seen.

In the next chapter, we'll explore the core archetypes and wounds of the inner child, so you can begin identifying these patterns in your clients - and perhaps in yourself too.

Chapter 4
Inner Child Archetypes & Wounds

"When this Child Within is not nurtured or allowed freedom of expression, a false or co-dependent self emerges."

Charles L. Whitfield

One of the most helpful ways to support clients through inner child healing is to understand the patterns and personalities that commonly emerge. Whilst every client is unique, many express their inner child through similar emotional themes or archetypes. These archetypes can help us identify the kinds of wounds that need healing, and how best to approach that healing in a session.

We'll also look at how these archetypes link to specific emotional wounds, such as rejection, abandonment, shame or unmet needs.

The Core Archetypes

There are seven common inner child archetypes that tend to show up in this work. They're not fixed roles, and clients may resonate or align with more than one, but they offer a useful way to understand the patterns and unmet needs that often linger beneath the surface.

One of the most frequently encountered is the **Wounded (or Innocent) Child**. This child carries the deep emotional pain caused by trauma, neglect or unmet needs. In adulthood, this archetype often appears as someone who feels overly sensitive or emotionally vulnerable, unable to trust and easily overwhelmed and unsure of their place in the world. Beneath the surface is often a history of betrayal or emotional abandonment that has never been soothed.

Closely related is the **Orphaned Child**, who holds the wound of abandonment and rejection. This child may have grown up feeling unseen, unloved or emotionally exiled. In adult life, these clients often experience attachment struggles, a persistent fear of being left or chronic feelings of loneliness, even when surrounded by people.

The **Magical Child** represents imagination and creativity, wonder and possibility. It's the part of us that still believes in hope and magic. When wounded, however, this child may have been dismissed, mocked or forced to 'grow up' too soon. Adults carrying this archetype might feel creatively blocked, uninspired by life, disconnected from pleasure or happiness, hesitant to dream or create a vision, or unable to express themselves freely. They've lost their spark.

Then there's the **Nature Child**, deeply connected to the natural world and sensory experience. This child finds comfort in trees, animals, textures or the rhythm of the seasons. When wounded or disconnected, the adult may feel lost, anxious, or unable to ground themselves, cut off from the calm and peace that once felt so natural.

The **Eternal Child** wants to stay in the world of innocence and playfulness. This can bring spontaneity and optimism, but may also create unwillingness to take on adult responsibilities or face reality. Clients with this pattern may avoid commitment, procrastinate or feel overwhelmed by the pressures of daily life. Their wound often stems from a fear of growing up, possibly due to the role models or experiences they had in childhood.

The **Needy Child** longs for the consistent love, attention, safety and reassurance they never received. As adults, these individuals may struggle with co-dependency, constantly seek approval or have a deep-seated fear that they are not enough. Their emotional deprivation often leaves them constantly striving for validation that seems just out of reach.

And last, but not least, the **Divine Child** carries a natural connection to something greater; a sense of inner light, purity, innocence, wisdom and a connection to the spiritual or sacred aspects of life. When this child is wounded, however, the adult may feel ashamed of who they truly are, be spiritually disconnected or convinced they are somehow flawed or unworthy. Adults carrying this kind of wound often struggle with low self-worth or a quiet ache for belonging, a sense that they're still looking for their place in the world, or for something that will finally feel like home.

Inner Child Healing and Hypnosis

These inner child archetypes aren't fixed or clinical labels. They're simply lenses; ways of understanding the emotional needs, coping strategies, and protective roles that formed in childhood.

Clients might strongly identify with one of these archetypes or find that several resonate. The value lies not in diagnosis, but in compassion; offering a way to meet the younger self with insight and care. We're simply offering a language for what they've carried all along.

Use these archetypes as a way to better understand the emotional energy behind their behaviours, beliefs and fears.

A moment from my journey

Looking back now, I can see that my magical child appeared very early. I was probably about five, lying in bed, when I saw the circus parade in my bedroom. Not in a dream, not in a story, but in full colour, wide awake. I remember the wonder of it: the tall ringmaster in a red coat and top hat, the elephants swaying gently as they passed, the lions, the tightrope walkers balancing so gracefully in the air; a whole parade of jugglers, acrobats and so much more, and the music. It was like the entire magic of the big top had somehow spilled into that little room.

But when I tried to share the experience, I was quickly shut down. I was told not to be silly, not to make things up. And just like that, something precious was dismissed. I see that moment as the beginning of my magical child retreating. The part of me that believed in possibility, that felt so connected to something bigger and more enchanted, learned it was safer to be quiet.

It's no wonder that years later, when I moved away and unexpectedly found myself in a spiritual circle, something quietly clicked. It felt like I'd come home. These people didn't dismiss or mock, they celebrated and encouraged intuition and that 'just knowing'. For the first time in years, I had permission to trust those deeper parts of myself again. And that's when my magical child began to stir and smile again. I rediscovered that part of me that had always known there was more to life than what could be explained.

Mapping Archetypes to Wounds

Understanding which inner child archetype is most present for your client can offer valuable guidance throughout the therapeutic process. When we're in tune with the emotional themes that define each archetype, we're better equipped to anticipate the client's emotional responses, choose the most supportive language, and guide them through imagery and suggestion that speaks directly to the part of them that needs healing.

By identifying the emotional themes behind a client's experience, you can begin to offer reflections that help them understand their patterns with more kindness and curiosity. This might sound like:

"I wonder if there's a younger part of you that felt left out or overlooked, like no one really saw you or listened. What do you think that part might need from you today?"

Or perhaps:

"Sometimes when we feel like we have to be perfect, it's a younger part of us trying to feel safe or accepted. I wonder what kind of reassurance that part might be longing for."

These kinds of invitations open the door to deeper understanding without pressure. They help the client stay connected to their own experience, without labelling it or making it wrong, and begin to meet it with compassion instead of shame. It also allows them to step into a more nurturing and conscious relationship with the younger part of themselves; a relationship that is no longer reactive, but responsive and loving.

As clients begin to name and recognise these inner parts, healing becomes less abstract. They're no longer 'overreacting,' 'too sensitive' or 'needy.' Instead, they're reconnecting with a part of themselves that once learned to survive without the support they truly needed. Your role is to honour that survival, while helping them explore new possibilities for emotional safety, belonging and wholeness.

A thought from me

Within you, there's a child who needs love, acceptance and healing. It still longs to be seen, heard, and held with compassion. That child may show up as sadness, anger, perfectionism or withdrawal, not to make life harder but as a way of asking for care. When we begin to recognise these younger parts for what they are - echoes of our earliest experiences - we create space for something powerful to unfold.

Healing starts with awareness, and deepens with love. Nurture that child and you don't just heal old wounds, you transform your life.

In the next chapter, we'll explore how to assess your clients' readiness for inner child work, and how to create a safe container for the vulnerable work ahead.

Chapter 5
Client Assessment & Readiness

"Whether we realize it or not, it is our woundedness, or how we cope with it, that dictates much of our behavior, shapes our social habits, and informs our ways of thinking about the world."

Gabor Maté

Before going straight into inner child healing, it's important to take a step back and consider whether a client is ready for this kind of deep emotional work. Hypnotherapy can open the door to vulnerable places in the subconscious, and that can lead to powerful change. But for the process to be truly helpful, the client needs to have the internal resources to manage what comes up along the way.

This chapter will help you identify:

- whether a client is emotionally and mentally prepared
- what to look for during early sessions
- how to support clients who aren't quite ready yet.

Assessing Emotional Readiness

Inner child healing often stirs emotional material that has been buried for a long time. For the work to be safe and effective, it's important to ensure that your client has enough emotional stability and resilience to engage with it.

You're looking for signs that the client can stay present when difficult feelings arise, process those emotions without becoming overwhelmed and soothe themselves in the time between sessions.

You might begin to explore this gently, using questions like, *"How do you usually cope when something emotional comes up?"* or *"Have you done any personal development or therapy work before?"* These kinds of questions give you a sense of their emotional range and capacity, how comfortable they are with reflection and whether they're used to working with their feelings.

It can also be helpful to ask something like, *"How do you take care of yourself when life feels challenging?"* Their answer may give you some insight into whether they have reliable strategies in place, or whether they might need a little more support in building emotional safety before going deeper.

Clients who are able to reflect on their experiences, name their emotions, and describe at least some way of looking after themselves are usually in a good position to begin this work. That doesn't mean they need to be emotionally 'together', just that they have a level of awareness and enough internal or external support to keep them steady.

Current Stability and Support Systems

Before beginning inner child work, it's also worth considering what else the client is holding in their life right now. If they're going through something intense, such as a bereavement, a relationship breakdown or recent trauma, they may need space to settle and stabilise before exploring deeper emotional work. Likewise, if they're living with active addiction, unmanaged mental health issues or are in crisis, this work may be too much without additional support in place.

You're not looking for perfection or emotional calm, just enough steadiness for them to engage with the process without becoming destabilised.

You might gently explore their current support system by asking something like, *"Because this work can bring things to the surface, it's important that you feel safe and supported - not just here, but in your life day to day. Who do you turn to for emotional support?"* This question gives you a sense of their external resources and whether they have friends, family or a community they can lean on.

It's also helpful to think about whether the client is in a place to attend and engage consistently. Life can be unpredictable but if they're finding it difficult to show up regularly, it might be a sign that this kind of work needs to wait until there's a little more space in their life, or a steadier routine to support it.

Signs a Client May Not Be Ready (Yet)

Even when a client says they want to do this work, there may be signs that the timing isn't quite right. That doesn't mean they're resistant or unwilling, it may simply mean they need more support, grounding or emotional regulation skills before moving into deeper healing.

You might notice that when childhood is mentioned, they quickly change the subject or brush it off. They may struggle to name or sit with difficult feelings, or they might focus heavily on logic and analysis as a way to stay in control. Sometimes, clients with limited insight into their own patterns, or those who have never done any reflective work before, need a softer starting point.

When this happens, it's not a failure, it's information!

Rather than push forward, this is a great opportunity to lay a stronger foundation. You can focus on building self-awareness, understanding of and ability to express emotions, and resilience. Sometimes this means beginning with sessions that strengthen the adult self; developing self-care strategies, emotional regulation tools and boundaries. All of this creates the safety and confidence needed to eventually meet the younger self inside.

With time, trust and support many clients who aren't quite ready at first will return to this work feeling more grounded and much more open to what it might bring.

Client Assessment & Readiness

A moment from my journey

I didn't understand the concept of emotional readiness when I first began my own healing journey. I thought wanting to feel better was enough. And in many ways, that motivation helped me take the first steps. But I quickly learned that healing isn't just about wanting change, it's also about having the support to hold yourself steady when the past begins to stir.

I started my healing in a safe space. It was a workshop where I'd got to know and trusted the leaders. There was a point where something deeply emotional made itself known. I wasn't expecting it, and although someone was holding the space for me, I wasn't quite ready or able to hold it for myself. I was left feeling raw and unsettled, not because anything had been done wrong, but because I hadn't yet developed the tools or self-awareness to integrate what had surfaced.

It took time. I had to learn how to trust myself, to slow things down and to understand that safety wasn't something I had to force, it was something I could grow. And when I was finally ready, the work went deeper in ways I could never have imagined.

That experience taught me something I never forgot: readiness isn't about being healed or having it all together. It's about having a strong enough foundation to begin meeting yourself with honesty and care.

Consent and Clarity

Inner child work can be profound, but it's also deeply personal. It's essential that clients understand what this process involves before you begin. That means offering clear and honest information, not just about the techniques but also about the emotional territory that might arise.

Let your client know that the work may bring up strong feelings, memories or unexpected emotional responses. Let them know they'll be guided gently and that they're always in control. Reassure them that nothing is forced and there is no pressure to remember anything specific or feel anything in particular.

You might say something like, *"This process can sometimes stir things that feel old or surprising. We'll take it at your pace, and you can pause or stop at any time. I'll be here with you throughout, and we'll check in regularly."*

Consent isn't something you get once and tick off, it's ongoing. A client may feel ready at the beginning of a session and then suddenly feel overwhelmed. That's okay. It's your job to stay present and responsive, giving them the space to feel safe and respected at every step.

When clients understand what to expect and still express a willingness to move forward, it's often a good sign that they're emotionally ready. And even if they decide to wait, the very act of having this conversation plants a seed. It tells the inner child, *"We're listening now, and we're taking care"*.

A thought from me

Inner child work doesn't begin with childhood memories. It begins with something more vital: the creation of safety. When a client feels stable and supported, the inner child starts to stir - not in fear, but with a sense of possibility. Trust builds gradually, forming a bridge between past and present. From there, the process can unfold in a way that feels steady and respectful. Healing isn't forced; it emerges when the time is right, when the client feels equipped to explore what's been carried quietly for so long.

In the next chapter, we'll explore how to create the kind of therapeutic space that allows deep healing work to happen, starting with physical safety, a calm and supportive presence, and compassionate, intentional language – words that reassure rather than re-traumatise.

Chapter 6
Creating a Safe Therapeutic Space

"People start to heal the moment they feel heard."

Cheryl Richardson

Inner child work opens a doorway into some of the most tender, vulnerable parts of a client's psyche. For the work to be effective, and for it to be safe, it must be done in an environment where clients feel completely accepted, held and free from judgement.

This chapter will explore:

- how to create emotional safety in your sessions
- the role of grounding and gentle language
- why boundaries and clear expectations matter

The Foundation: Safety Before Strategy

The most effective inner child work doesn't begin with a script, it begins with feeling safe. Clients may say they want to do the work - and often they do - but unless they feel safe with you and safe within themselves, their subconscious may hold back.

That sense of safety doesn't come from scripts or techniques. It comes from your tone, your presence, and the consistency you show up with. Clients need to feel they won't be judged, rushed, or pushed into anything before they're ready.

You can begin to build this trust through the little things; by using warm and gentle language, by letting the client set the pace, and by honouring even the smallest emotional expression. Sometimes, it's just about sitting with someone in their discomfort and letting them know they're not alone.

Let your client know from the beginning that they're in control. Remind them that their reactions, even if surprising or unfamiliar, are valid and welcome. When someone feels seen and accepted at that level the defences start to soften. And from there, real healing becomes possible.

A moment from my journey

When I first began this work, I remember wondering if I could really hold space for someone else's pain without being pulled under by it. I had done a lot of personal development already, but inner child work was different because it asked something deeper of me.

I'm thinking back to a moment from my early days as a therapist when someone sat across from me, eyes brimming with tears, their words faltering as they tried to speak about a childhood memory they hadn't voiced in decades. I didn't know what to say. So I said very little. I just stayed with them. I remember placing a box of tissues gently within reach and softening my expression to match the softness of the space I hoped to offer. I remember the air felt still, like we were holding something sacred.

Afterwards, they told me they felt safe, not because of anything I did, but because I didn't try to fix them. I hadn't filled the silence or reached for a clever phrase. I'd simply stayed. That was the moment I truly understood what holding space meant.

It's easy to forget how rare that kind of presence can be. But for our clients' inner child - and for our own - it can be the very thing that makes healing possible.

The Power of Language

When we work with the inner child words matter, often more than we realise. The words we use as hypnotherapists are incredibly powerful. We are speaking directly to the subconscious, and subtle shifts in tone and language can make a huge difference. Essentially, we either open the door to healing or reinforce old fears and defences.

Using more gentle, non-directive language helps create a sense of emotional safety. This might mean softening suggestions with phrases like, *"you might like to"* or *"if it feels right, you could"* rather than *"you will"* or *"you must"*. These subtle shifts help clients feel they're still in control, even in a deeply relaxed state.

It's also important to use clean language; words that don't impose meaning or assume details. Developed in the 1980s by psychologist David Grove, Clean Language is widely used in talk therapies to help clients explore their internal experience without influence or suggestion from the therapist. It uses simple, neutral questions that reflect the client's own words, allowing their subconscious to lead the process.

Rather than interpreting, reframing, or introducing imagery, the therapist stays with the client's language and experience, asking questions like,

- *"And when you say [client's word], what kind of [client's word] is that?"*
- *"And where is that [client's word]?"*
- *"Where are you now?"*
- *"What can you see?"*

Clean language respects the client's internal world and leaves space for their unique experience to emerge, without us unintentionally shaping it. Instead of saying, *"You see your younger self sitting in a dark corner"* and leading them, we might say, *"Perhaps there's an image that comes to mind, maybe of a younger you – what do you see? How do you feel?"* This allows the client's subconscious to reveal what it needs to, without pressure or influence.

This approach is particularly valuable in inner child work, where the therapist's assumptions - even well-intentioned ones - can subtly shape the client's journey. Clean language helps ensure that the images, emotions and metaphors that arise are truly the client's own, making the experience more meaningful and trustworthy.

Metaphor can also be a powerful ally. Imagery like 'a soft blanket', 'a warm light' or 'a safe place inside' speaks to the nervous system in ways that logical explanations can't. The subconscious responds well to symbols, and when those symbols represent comfort, safety, and belonging, they help the inner child feel held and welcomed.

Throughout the session, you can also use reassuring phrases to anchor the client's experience. Phrases such as: *"You're doing really well, and I'm right here with you." "You're in control at every moment." "You can come back to your safe place whenever you need to."*

These small, consistent signals let the subconscious know it's okay to relax, to explore and to begin healing, one moment at a time.

Grounding Techniques

Even in a deeply relaxed state, it's essential that clients feel anchored and safe. Grounding techniques can help if emotions rise suddenly, if the client starts to dissociate, or if they become overwhelmed during or after hypnosis.

It's a good idea to introduce grounding methods early in your work together so the client becomes familiar with them and feels confident using them both inside and outside of session.

Some grounding techniques include:

- **Safe place visualisation** – guiding the client to imagine a calming environment, often filled with comforting sensory details. This becomes a mental "anchor" they can return to anytime they need reassurance.

- **Body awareness** – inviting the client to notice where their body meets the chair or floor, or to feel the weight of their feet on the ground. This helps bring them back into the here and now.

- **Breath focus** – encouraging slow, intentional breathing. You might guide them to inhale for a count of four and exhale for six, allowing the longer out-breath to activate the parasympathetic nervous system and promote calm.

- **Sensory grounding** – asking the client to mentally, or openly, name five things they can see, four they can touch or feel, three they can hear, two they can smell, and one they can taste. This technique, often used in trauma work, gently guides their awareness back to the present moment.

Introducing these techniques as part of your early sessions helps the client feel safe enough to go deeper in future work. They become tools the client can use not just in hypnosis, but in everyday life whenever emotional intensity arises.

Boundaries and Expectations

Boundaries aren't barriers, they're containers. In inner child work, clear boundaries help create a sense of structure and safety, which in turn allows the deeper emotional work to unfold more freely. When clients know what to expect they're less likely to feel anxious, confused or unsure of their place in the process.

From the very beginning, it's helpful to be clear about how sessions are structured, how long they will last and what kind of contact (if any) is appropriate between appointments. This protects your time and energy but, more importantly, it models healthy relational dynamics - something many clients may never have experienced before.

It's also worth setting expectations around the work itself. Clients often come into therapy thinking they'll either 'fix the issue' or experience a big emotional breakthrough. You can gently reframe this by explaining that inner child healing is layered and non-linear. Some sessions may feel calm and reflective, while others stir deeper emotion. Both are valuable. Both are valid.

You might say: *"This kind of work unfolds gently. It's okay if you don't have all the answers or if things come up between sessions. You're welcome to jot them down and bring them with you next time, but we'll keep the deeper processing for inside the session, where it's held and supported."*

This kind of container gives the inner child something they may never have had - consistency, emotional safety and someone who honours their pace. When a client feels that, the healing doesn't have to be rushed, it simply begins.

Non-Judgemental Presence

Perhaps more than anything else, what clients need from us during inner child work is presence. Not expertise, not solutions but a steady, compassionate presence that says 'you're safe here' and 'you're allowed to feel what you feel.'

For many clients, this may be the first time they've truly felt seen without being analysed, corrected or hurried. That in itself is healing. When a therapist can sit with a client in silence, in sadness, in uncertainty, and still offer warmth and acceptance, the inner child begins to relax. The nervous system softens. Trust grows.

This isn't about doing nothing. It's about doing less of what the world has already done to them - interrupting, dismissing, intellectualising - and more of what they've always needed; someone who listens, someone who stays.

You don't have to have the perfect response. You don't need to fix their feelings. Your calm, grounded presence is enough. The way you look at them with kindness, the way you honour what arises without judgement, that's where the healing begins.

It's in this quiet, gentle space that the inner child learns something new, *'You are welcome. Just as you are.'*

Creating a Safe Therapeutic Space

✧ ✧ ✧ ✧ ✧ ✧ ✧

A thought from me

You don't need to have the perfect script, the ideal technique, or even a plan for what comes next. What matters most is your presence. To sit with another human being, free of judgement or agenda, is one of the rarest gifts we can offer.

For many clients, safety has never felt like this; unearned, unquestioned, quietly offered without conditions. Your willingness to stay, to witness their story without rushing to reshape it, is what allows healing to begin.

Because when someone feels safe in your presence, truly safe, they begin to believe they can be safe with themselves. And that changes everything.

✧ ✧ ✧ ✧ ✧ ✧ ✧

In the next chapter, we'll explore how to sensitively navigate resistance. Because, even in the safest space, the subconscious might still try to protect the client from going too deep too quickly.

Chapter 7
Navigating & Framing Resistance

"What we resist persists."

Carl Jung

Even when a client feels ready and safe, resistance can still show up. Resistance is not a sign of failure or avoidance, often it's a sign that we're getting close to something important. Something the subconscious has been protecting for a long time.

Rather than treating resistance as a problem to be fixed, it can be helpful to approach it with curiosity and compassion. When we see it as a message rather than a barrier, we open the door to deeper understanding.

Recognising Resistance

Resistance doesn't always look or sound like *"I don't want to do this."* It can be subtle, quiet and often unconscious. You might notice your client overthinking, rationalising, or shifting quickly into humour. Sometimes they might struggle to access memories, emotions, or sensations. Others may appear tired, distracted or disconnected during visualisation. They may miss sessions or arrive late, even when they're engaged with the work.

All of these are forms of self-protection. They make perfect sense when you consider that the inner child may have spent decades hiding, staying quiet or retreating to feel safe.

A moment from my journey

There was a time I thought I was making no progress at all. I was going to workshops, reading the books, I kept turning up, but something inside me held back. I remember one particular retreat where everyone else seemed to be having big emotional releases and getting powerful insights - and yet I felt nothing. Just a dull, frozen numbness.

Part of me was frustrated. Another part felt broken. I remember walking home on my own that evening and thinking, "What's wrong with me? Why can't I feel what they're feeling?"

It took me a long time to understand that my resistance was a feeling. That frozen part wasn't a sign of failure; it was a sign of protection. I'd spent so long holding everything in, putting on a brave face, surviving what life threw at me, that of course it wasn't going to melt overnight. That numbness was a gatekeeper. A fiercely loyal part of me saying, "Not yet. Not until it's safe."

Looking back now, I see how tender and wise that part

was. It wasn't until I stopped trying to break it down, and began listening instead, that it began to soften. That was when the real healing started.

Why Resistance Arises

Resistance is not the enemy; it's simply the nervous system doing its job. It can arise when the client believes that facing something painful will be too overwhelming. It may stem from a learned fear of vulnerability or a history of being shamed for expressing emotion. In this context, resistance is not a block. It is a signal. A part of the client is saying, *"I'm not quite ready."* Our job is to listen to that message, not override it.

Understanding Resistance as Protection

What we often label as resistance is rarely defiance or unwillingness. More often, it's protection. A part of the subconscious doing exactly what it was designed to do: keep the person safe. When a client hesitates, deflects or disconnects during inner child work, it may be because a protective part of them is scanning for danger. Perhaps they've opened up in the past and been met with shame, rejection or indifference. Perhaps their inner child has learned that being visible equals being vulnerable. In these moments, rather than pushing forward, it helps to gently honour the wisdom of that resistance. It exists for a reason. And when we treat it with respect rather than frustration, it often begins to soften on its own.

Strategies for Navigating Resistance

In these moments, slowing down can be more effective than pressing forward. You might stay with lighter material, use metaphor, or help the client reconnect with their safe place. For example, you could invite them to explore an image: *"If this feeling was a wall, what might it look like? Is there anything on the other side?"*

When the client feels in control, they feel safer. Remind them they can pause at any time. They do not need to go further than feels comfortable. That simple reassurance can make all the difference.

It can also be helpful to gently acknowledge the protective part directly. You might invite the client to ask, *"What are you trying to protect me from?"* or *"What do you need from me right now?"* Often, just recognising this part's good intentions allows it to relax.

Clients may worry they're doing it wrong. You can reassure them, *"There's no right way to do this. Whatever you're feeling, or not feeling, is okay."*

And if nothing is happening, you might say, *"Even if it feels like nothing is happening, your mind is still listening. Still responding in its own way."*

The most powerful shift sometimes comes not from pushing through resistance, but from reframing it as wisdom. What looks like hesitation is often self-preservation. What appears to be avoidance may be a carefully learned survival skill. What looks like failure is pacing.

Navigating & Framing Resistance

You might say something like, *"It sounds like your mind is doing what it has always done. Trying to take care of you. Maybe we can thank it for that, and ask if it's willing to let us see a little further. Only if it feels okay."*

When resistance is met with kindness instead of force, it often begins to melt. The client learns they don't have to brace or hide any longer. And the inner child learns that vulnerability can be safe; it's finally safe to be seen.

A thought from me

Sometimes the most resistant parts of us are the ones that need love the most. Like a frightened animal hiding in the shadows, they've learned to protect themselves by staying small, silent or guarded. These parts aren't trying to block the healing; they're standing watch at the gates, making sure the pain doesn't slip through again.

When we stop trying to push past them and instead sit quietly nearby, offering safety and stillness, they may begin to inch forward. Not because we forced them, but because they finally feel safe enough to be seen. In that moment, healing begins - not with a breakthrough, but with a relaxing of old defences.

In the next chapter, we turn to the teachings of Louise Hay, whose work offers a compassionate path toward healing the inner child through acceptance, affirmation and emotional safety.

Chapter 8
Louise Hay and the Inner Child

"You have been criticising yourself for years and it hasn't worked. Try approving of yourself and see what happens."

Louise Hay

Louise Hay was a pioneer in the field of self-healing. She began her career as a metaphysical teacher and author in the 1970s, and over time became known worldwide for her work on the mind-body connection, the power of affirmations, and emotional healing. Her best-known book, *You Can Heal Your Life*, sold millions of copies and helped to popularise the idea that our thoughts and emotions influence our physical and emotional wellbeing.

Although not a therapist in the traditional sense, Louise had an extraordinary gift for helping people reconnect with themselves. Her approach was simple, intuitive and full of heart. She believed that most of the pain people carry comes from childhood; moments when we were criticised, dismissed, hurt or ignored. Her work centred on helping people replace those old, harmful messages with new ones based on self-love and acceptance.

Many elements of her work reflect hypnotic structure and principles. Her use of visualisation, positive suggestion, affirmations and rhythm in language were all consistent with the ways we work in hypnosis. This makes her approach naturally adaptable for hypnotherapists working with inner child healing.

For many people, myself included, Louise Hay's work offers a gentle and heartfelt introduction to the idea of inner child healing. Her teachings reminded us that the part of us who still feels afraid or unworthy does not need fixing. It needs kindness.

A moment from my journey

I often say Louise Hay saved my life.

And it's true - Louise Hay's work changed my life. Completely. It was the beginning of my own healing. It was the first time I truly began to understand that the pain I carried wasn't because something was wrong with me, but because my inner child had never been shown the love she deserved

It came at a time when I felt broken and uncertain of my place in the world. Her voice, her words, and the simple practice of affirming myself began to soften something inside me.

The biggest shift came when I realised that I was attracting many of the things that were happening in my life, not because I deserved them but because I didn't even like myself, let alone love myself.

That understanding changed everything. It helped me begin to relate to myself with more compassion, and opened the door to a very different way of living.

It helped me begin to care for myself, rather than constantly criticise or abandon myself. It also showed me the power of suggestion, of language, and of deep emotional safety.

That understanding and practice later became the foundation for the work I now do with others.

Louise believed that many of our current problems are rooted in childhood messages we absorbed and repeated to ourselves over time. These messages became our beliefs, and our beliefs shaped our behaviour, our relationships, and even our health. The invitation she offered was simple: if we could begin to change those messages, we could change how we felt about ourselves, and over time, change our lives.

At the heart of her work was the belief that we all have an inner child who needs to be heard, seen, and loved. She showed people how to offer that love themselves, often for the first time.

The Power of Affirmations

Affirmations were central to Louise's teachings. Not just as surface-level positive thinking, but as a way to speak to the younger parts of ourselves who learned something untrue. Perhaps they learned they were not good enough, or that love had to be earned, or that emotions were unsafe. An affirmation like "*I am safe now*" or "*I am loved and I belong*" can land deeply when it is offered gently and repeatedly, especially in a relaxed hypnotic state.

A key point with any affirmation is, for it to be effective, it should be positive, personal and in the present tense. Our subconscious mind responds most powerfully to what we affirm as true now, not in some distant or hypothetical future. If we keep saying something 'will be', then on a subconscious level, it remains just out of reach. Saying 'I am' is far more empowering than 'I will be', even if it doesn't feel fully true yet.

For example, *"I am learning to trust myself"* is more effective than *"One day I will trust myself"*, because it affirms a shift already in progress. Likewise, *"I am open to healing"* lands more powerfully than *"I hope to heal"*. Affirmations like *"I am safe now"*, *"I am allowed to rest"*, or *"I am becoming more at ease with myself each day"* help the mind create new internal pathways, grounded in the present moment.

Hypnotherapy gives these affirmations a deeper channel. In trance, the critical mind quiets down, allowing new messages to settle into the subconscious. This is why combining Louise's style of affirmation with hypnosis is so effective. Clients are not simply repeating empty phrases. They are receiving emotional reassurance in a state where it can be accepted.

The Power of Mirror Work

One of Louise's most famous tools is Mirror Work. She encouraged people to look into a mirror, make eye contact with themselves and speak loving words. This can be deeply emotional. For some, it is the first time they have truly seen themselves with compassion. For others, it brings up resistance, discomfort or grief.

Mirror work can be a powerful practice to explore in or around inner child sessions. You might guide a client to imagine meeting their younger self in a mirror. They can offer a kind word or simply stand with them, allowing that connection to form. You can also suggest mirror work as a between-session practice, especially for clients who are beginning to develop self-trust and self-compassion.

Responsibility

Another key principle in Louise's work is personal responsibility. She didn't mean that we should accept blame for what happened or the way we feel. Instead, she invited people to recognise that while they may not be responsible for what happened to them, they are now responsible for their healing. This empowers the adult self to show up for the inner child, rather than continuing to wait for someone else to do it.

The Power of Forgiveness

She also emphasised the power of forgiveness. Not as something forced or rushed, but as a way of releasing the emotional burden of the past. Forgiveness is not about condoning what's been done to you, or what you may have done to someone else. It's choosing not to carry the pain for ever and setting yourself free from the pain of resentment. So, when a client is ready, forgiveness can become a turning point.

Louise Hay's work may appear deceptively simple but it taps into something really quite magical. It speaks to the inner child in a language they can understand. Kindness. Reassurance. Permission. These qualities are often missing in traditional therapeutic settings, yet they are vital in healing the wounds of the past.

Key Principles of Louise Hay's Inner Child Approach

- The inner child needs to be loved, not fixed. Louise often said, "You've been criticising yourself for years and it hasn't worked. Try approving of yourself and see what happens." At the heart of her message was that your inner child is not broken, they are waiting to be loved.
- Affirmations are a form of healing. Affirmations were central to her teachings. She taught that our thoughts shape our reality and that repeating positive, loving thoughts helps to overwrite the painful messages we absorbed growing up. In hypnotherapy, affirmations act as positive suggestions. When spoken and repeated in a hypnotic state, they sink into the subconscious - which is exactly what we do with hypnosis. Saying "I am safe now" or "I am worthy of love" in trance helps the client absorb it emotionally, not just intellectually.

- Mirror work. Louise often asked people to look in the mirror, make eye contact with themselves, and say something kind or loving. It sounds simple, but for many people this is incredibly emotional. For some, it's the first time they've ever really *seen* themselves with compassion. Mirror work is a powerful addition to hypnotherapy. Clients can be encouraged to visualise looking into a mirror and speaking to their inner child, or hearing their inner child speak to them.
- Forgiveness and emotional responsibility. Louise taught that we are not responsible for what others did to us, but we *are* responsible for our healing. She emphasised forgiveness; not to excuse others but to release ourselves. This aligns well with inner child work, where clients often carry shame, resentment or guilt that needs to be released.

Bringing these principles into hypnotherapy sessions can be as simple as weaving affirmations into a deepener or visualisation. It might involve inviting the client to place a hand on their heart, or to imagine speaking gently to their younger self. It can also show up as the language you use throughout your session. Are your words soft, inviting, spacious? Do they echo the messages the inner child most needs to hear?

Growth Beyond the Session

Even outside of hypnosis, you can offer clients Louise's tools as part of their self-care. Encourage them to choose an affirmation that feels right. Suggest a daily moment of mirror work, even if just for a few seconds. These are not just exercises. They are practices of reparenting and reconnection.

Repetition is key. In and out of hypnosis, affirmations work by gently replacing old beliefs. Their power lies in their simplicity, their consistency, and the emotional resonance they carry when offered with care and sincerity. At their core, affirmations are repeated suggestions which is, after all, one of the fundamental principles of hypnotherapy.

A thought from me

This chapter isn't just included because it fits, it's here because Louise Hay's work changed my life and continues to shape the way I work. Her words offered me a way back to myself when I felt lost, and her simple heartfelt tools are still among the most powerful I've ever used.

Affirmations aren't just words. They are small, consistent acts of reparenting - small steps that help to untangle old beliefs and offer the inner child something new: love, safety, and a different truth. When spoken with sincerity, they soften the echoes of old wounds and rewrite the stories we once believed about ourselves.

Healing doesn't have to be complicated. It can begin with a phrase, a glance in the mirror, a whisper of self-approval. Over time, those small acts become a steady rhythm that leads us home.

In hypnotherapy, these tools offer a practical way to

support the inner child where it matters most. You can use it for yourself as well, and it's a gift I pass on to every client and student who crosses my path.

✧ ✧ ✧ ✧ ✧ ✧ ✧

In the next chapter, we'll explore core techniques for guiding clients into inner child healing using hypnotherapy.

Chapter 9
Core Hypnotherapy Techniques for Inner Child Healing

"The subconscious mind is like a tape player. Until you change the tape, it will not change."

Bruce Lipton

Hypnosis provides a uniquely supportive space to access the subconscious mind, where much of our inner child's pain, protection and unmet needs are held. It can help clients build trust with those younger parts, release emotional burdens and begin to rewire limiting beliefs. This chapter outlines core techniques that can be used across different stages of the healing journey.

Each of these techniques should be approached with flexibility. No two clients are the same, and the inner child may respond differently depending on the day, the state of the nervous system or the emotional readiness of the adult self.

Move through these stages with patience, understanding, and a willingness to change direction if the client resists or needs something different. Always follow the client's pace.

A moment from my journey

I remember listening to a guided visualisation. Nothing dramatic happened, just a feeling, a flicker of an image. And then, suddenly, I was with a much younger version of myself. She looked small, uncertain and almost surprised that I'd noticed her. I didn't know what to say. But I stayed with her.

That simple moment - being present without needing to fix or analyse - became a turning point. That was when I realised that healing wasn't about doing something to the inner child. It was about being with her. Offering her the safety and presence she'd always needed.

It was also when I began to understand how powerful this could be. And later, I started experimenting using what I'd learned, both in and out of hypnosis. Using it not as a tool for control or correction, but as a doorway to relationship, to reconnection and to self-belief and self-compassion.

That visualisation certainly didn't fix everything, but it opened something up. A new kind of listening. A new way of being with myself. And it's the same kind of space I now aim to hold for every client I work with.

Safe Place Visualisation

Before beginning any deep inner child work, it's vital to establish a sense of internal safety. A safe place visualisation offers the client a personal, emotional refuge that they can return to at any point, during or outside of trance. This internal space might be real or imagined, but it needs to be somewhere peaceful, comforting and just for them.

You can introduce this early in the therapeutic relationship and use it regularly as an anchor. Clients often return to their safe place automatically when emotional material arises, and it gives both the child and the adult self a felt sense of choice and control. Over time, it becomes a trusted foundation for deeper work.

This technique is also helpful when clients feel overwhelmed, disconnected, or uncertain. Simply guiding them back to their safe place can re-establish calm and stability without interrupting the flow of the session.

Age Regression

Age regression is a powerful way of accessing the original imprint of a belief or emotional pattern. In the context of inner child healing, it can gently guide the client back to the time when a wound was formed, so it can be witnessed, processed, and softened.

The key is to approach regression with care and clean language, allowing the subconscious to reveal what's ready, without suggesting, leading or interpreting. Clients may recall clear events, vague impressions, or seemingly unrelated images. All of these are valid.

It's important to remind clients that what surfaces may or may not be literal memory. That doesn't reduce its value. The experience is symbolic and emotional, and it speaks the language of the inner world.

Some clients arrive at regression naturally through free association or emotional imagery. Others benefit from a gentle age progression or drifting back through time to an earlier time, to a time when the feeling or pattern first began. However the journey unfolds, regression should never be forced. Always make sure they are emotionally ready, grounded, and have a way to return to safety if the need arises.

Meeting the Inner Child

One of the most moving experiences in hypnotherapy is when a client meets their inner child, perhaps for the first time. This meeting is not about rescuing or fixing. It is about just being there. About seeing, hearing and gently connecting with the part of themselves that may have felt alone for a very long time.

You might begin by inviting the client to visualise a scene from the past or simply ask, *"If a younger part of you were to appear now, what might they look like?"* The response might be vivid or subtle. Sometimes it's a clear image. Sometimes it's just a feeling or a sense of age or energy.

Encourage the client to approach this younger self with warmth and respect. Let the child set the tone. Sometimes they want to talk. Sometimes they just want to be noticed. Either way, the connection begins to restore a relationship that had likely been neglected or severed.

It's important to observe what the child shows through posture, expression or surroundings. These often hold meaning. And rather than analysing them, you can simply reflect back and allow the client to respond with curiosity and care.

Inner Dialogue

Once a connection has been made, you might begin to facilitate a conversation between the adult and the child. This is often where deeper healing begins. Inner dialogue gives voice to needs, fears, and longings that may never have been expressed out loud.

The adult self could ask questions like, *"What do you need from me?"* or *"What have you been holding all this time?"* And the child can speak in their own way, through words, emotion or imagery.

As the therapist, your role is to hold the space, support the flow and offer gentle guidance if needed. Avoid interpreting or pushing for clarity. Just allow the process to be organic.

Sometimes the dialogue brings relief, as the child feels truly heard. Sometimes it surfaces grief or anger. All of this is welcome. The adult self, if ready, can offer comfort, reassurance, and validation; gifts the child may never have received at the time.

Reparenting

Reparenting is at the heart of inner child healing. It involves the adult self stepping into a nurturing, protective, understanding and supportive role that may have been missing from or inconsistent in the client's early life.

Through hypnosis, the client can begin to give their inner child what was missing; safety, approval, affection, boundaries, or unconditional love. This can be done through visualisation, symbolic action such as wrapping the child in a blanket, holding them or simply by being present.

You might invite the client to imagine saying words the child needed to hear, or offering a gesture of comfort, such as holding their hand or sitting quietly beside them. These moments can be deeply emotional and therapeutically valuable, even without words.

It's also helpful to remind the client that reparenting is not a one-off act. It's a relationship. A growing connection between parts of themselves that may need time, consistency, and ongoing care.

Integration Techniques

After deep inner work, integration is an important part of the process. Clients may well feel a little open, unsettled or emotionally raw after connecting with their inner child. Integration techniques help them return to the here and now feeling more grounded, steady and whole.

You might close the session by guiding the adult and child into a shared place; a place that feels feel safe and supportive for both of them. Or you might suggest an image of the child stepping into the heart, the body or another symbolic space where they are welcomed and held.

Some clients respond well to symbolic objects; a glowing light, a soft blanket, a key or a small box that the child can rest in when not needed consciously. These metaphors give the subconscious a place to store the connection safely between sessions.

It's also useful to offer a few simple self-care prompts. Clients might like to journal after the session, place a comforting item on their bedside table or speak to their inner child with kindness during daily routines.

Integration reminds the client that the session is just one part of the process. The relationship with their inner child doesn't end when they leave the room. It continues, gradually unfolding over time.

This work may feel subtle, but it often creates a ripple effect. Clients might describe feeling lighter, more grounded or unexpectedly emotional in the days that follow. That's healing at work. It settles in and takes place beneath the surface.

A note on self-hypnosis for clients

While self-hypnosis can be a valuable resource for building emotional regulation, confidence, or relaxation, I approach it with caution when working with inner child themes. Not all clients feel safe revisiting early memories or emotions without the support of a therapist present. For this reason, I don't routinely teach self-hypnosis during early inner child work, especially where trauma may be involved. However, once the client has built enough internal safety and connection with their younger self, techniques such as visualisation or positive suggestion may be introduced in a structured and supportive way.

A thought from me

Hypnosis is never about fixing the client. Here, it's about guiding them into a space where they can finally hear their inner child, perhaps for the very first time. Then they can fix themselves.

Because in that space, change doesn't come from doing more, it comes from listening more deeply. From allowing what's been buried to be seen, heard and held with compassion. When the client connects with those forgotten parts, healing begins to happen not through force but through presence.

That's the quiet power of this work; helping someone find the strength they didn't know they had in the voice they'd almost forgotten was theirs.

In the next chapter, we'll explore advanced techniques for clients who are ready to go beyond the basics and work with more layered emotional themes and integrate at a different level.

Chapter 10
Advanced Techniques for Deeper Healing

"The body remembers what the mind forgets."

Jacob Levy Moreno

As the relationship between the adult self and the inner child begins to strengthen, deeper layers of healing become possible. Clients often reach a point where the initial reconnection has been made, and the protective parts no longer need to be so active. This is where more advanced approaches could be introduced; methods that support emotional repair and self-trust, and help create lasting integration.

This kind of work is not about doing more, going deeper for the sake of it, or trying to achieve a breakthrough. It is about listening more carefully, observing what wants to emerge, and choosing techniques that gently support the client in becoming more whole.

Healing doesn't always move in a straight line. Some sessions will feel expansive and affirming. Others may seem quieter, or even uncertain. These fluctuations are part of the process. The techniques offered in this chapter are tools, not requirements. They are available when the time feels right, once the client has more emotional resources, is stable, and ready to go deeper.

Somatic Memory Retrieval

Trauma, especially developmental trauma, often lives in the body. Long before we can put experiences into words, the body records sensations – perhaps anxiety, tightness, flinching, stillness, or numbness – which reflect how we learned to survive.

In hypnosis, somatic memory retrieval doesn't mean reliving trauma. It means helping the client notice what their body remembers. You might guide them to tune into a feeling in the chest, the stomach or the throat, and ask what age or moment it connects to. This awareness can be powerful, especially when approached gently and without expectation.

Supporting the client to notice bodily sensations with compassion, rather than fear, helps release held tension. A trembling hand, a sense of pressure, or a sudden need to shrink back can all be meaningful responses. The goal is not to interpret but to listen. Often, simply naming what the body is holding allows something to shift.

Parts or Ego State Therapy

As inner child healing progresses, more distinct parts of the self often begin to emerge. These may include the protector, the critic, the rebel, the perfectionist or other identities shaped by childhood experiences.

Parts therapy provides a framework for helping these inner voices feel heard and understood. When we invite dialogue between the adult self and these ego states, we often uncover the beliefs and needs that are driving behaviour. For example, the inner critic might be trying to prevent humiliation. The perfectionist may be trying to avoid rejection.

Rather than suppressing these parts, we offer them a seat at the table. You might ask, *"What does this part need?"* or *"What is it afraid will happen if it lets go?"*

As rapport grows, the client learns to bring leadership to their internal system. The adult self becomes the calm centre. Over time, this integration supports emotional regulation, self-trust and a deeper sense of wholeness.

Imaginary Rescripting

Imaginary rescripting allows the client to rewrite painful memories, not to erase them but to offer the younger self what was missing. It's a gentle process of re-imagining a past scene through the eyes of the adult self, bringing in understanding, support and choice.

You might guide a client to recall a difficult moment and then invite their adult self to step into that memory. What would they say? What would they change? Could they stop the event, remove the child or bring someone safe into the scene?

This process can sometimes be profoundly healing. The subconscious often responds to imagined safety as if it were real. The adult may perhaps feel a new sense of empowerment or closure. The child learns that what happened wasn't their fault, and that it's not still happening.

Timeline Work

Timeline work supports integration by helping the client organise and make sense of their emotional history. It can be used to track the development of a belief, to observe recurring patterns, or to highlight moments of resilience.

In hypnosis, you might invite the client to stand on a timeline and notice what arises at different points. They can observe from a distance or step into certain moments to explore them further. Some clients find it helpful to anchor empowering experiences alongside painful ones, creating a more balanced view of their past.

Timeline work also helps prepare for the future. You might guide the client to walk forward and visit a version of themselves who feels confident, connected or free from a particular pattern or feeling. These future-self visualisations can be very motivating and supportive.

A moment from my journey

By the time I began exploring some of these deeper techniques myself, I had already met and comforted my inner child many times. But there came a point where I realised something more was needed. Not more intensity but more listening. It wasn't a dramatic breakthrough, but it was cathartic. It was a quiet noticing, a change in how I related to the parts of me that had once felt too messy or too much.

I was journalling after a particularly emotional session, and I wrote a letter not to my inner child, but from her to me. The words flowed with a kind of raw honesty I hadn't expected. In her voice, I heard the ache of things never said, but also the courage to speak at last. That small act changed something. It wasn't about analysing but acknowledging what she said, responding with care, and letting her know I was really there.

That experience taught me that deeper healing doesn't always come from doing more. Sometimes, it comes from allowing space for what's buried to come to the surface - not to be fixed, but to be met with love.

Creative Expression

Not all healing happens through words. Sometimes drawing, writing, movement or symbolic acts allow the inner child to speak in a different language.

Clients may want to draw their inner child, write a letter to them, or from them, or create a simple ritual that honours a past version of themselves. These forms of expression can bypass resistance and reveal insights that verbal processing alone might miss.

You might suggest journalling after sessions, placing a small token somewhere visible to remind them of their progress, or even using simple breath and movement to embody a more nurturing state. These small acts help bridge the gap between inner work and everyday life.

Integration

At this stage, integration becomes less about technique and more about consistency. The client is learning to live in relationship with themselves; to check in, to listen, to respond. They are building a life where the inner child is no longer hidden or dismissed but welcomed.

Advanced work is not always dramatic. In fact, the most significant shifts often happen quietly. A moment of self-forgiveness. A pause before reacting. A new sense of ease in the body. These are the signs that the healing is landing.

As a hypnotherapist, your role is to hold the space for these transformations. Not to rush them, but to recognise and support them when they appear. This is integration in its truest sense. Not a final destination but a steady return to wholeness.

A thought from me

Sometimes healing doesn't come from the words we speak, but from the images that rise, the feelings we release, or the quiet moments when something finally shifts. It might be a sigh, a tear, a sensation easing in the body; something subtle, yet profoundly meaningful. These moments often arrive without fanfare, but they are the ones that linger. They remind us that healing is not always loud or logical.

Sometimes, it's what happens in the silence, when we allow ourselves to feel without judgement, to see without turning away, and to be present with whatever shows up. That's when real integration begins - not just in the mind, but in the whole self.

Next, we'll explore how to guide clients through a multi-session journey of healing, with a structured framework you can adapt to different client needs.

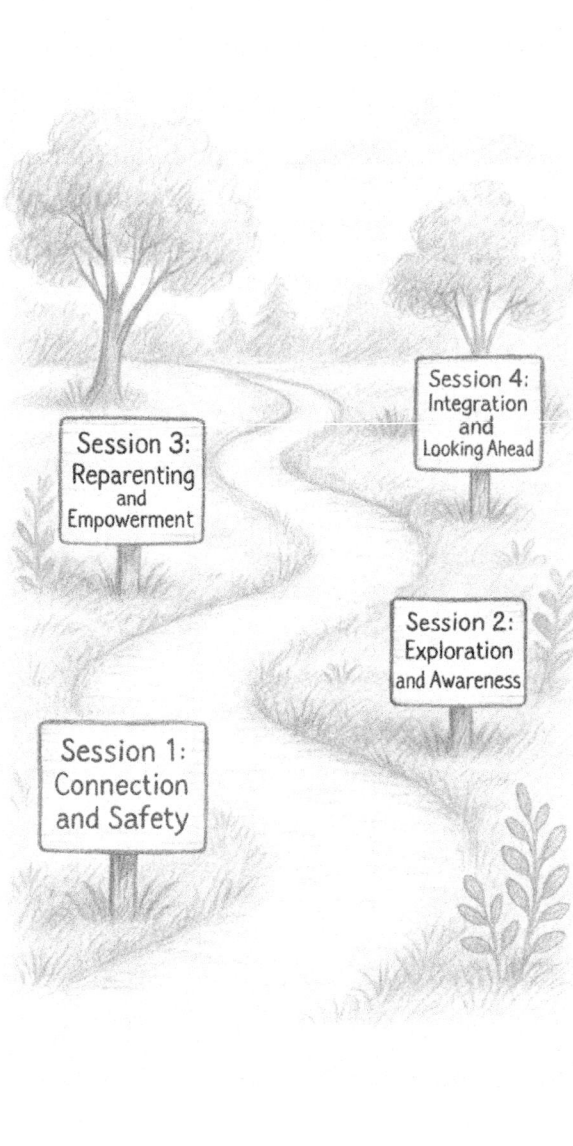

Chapter 11
Structuring a Multi-Session Healing Framework

"The journey of a thousand miles begins with a single step."

Lao Tzu

Every client's journey will look a little different, but having a flexible structure in place can be helpful for both client and therapist. It brings a sense of direction and container for the work, helping to pace the sessions, support emotional safety and avoid overwhelming the client by going too deep too quickly.

A loose framework allows for progression from initial connection to deeper emotional work and ultimately integration, while giving you plenty of scope to adjust based on the client's emotional readiness, needs and responses.

What follows is a suggested three to four session structure that can be adapted for shorter or longer programmes of work.

These are only my suggestions based on my own experience and practice. As a therapist, you develop your own style and language over time, and this is no exception. It's important to make it your own.

Session 1: Connection and Safety

Objective: Establish rapport with the inner child and lay the foundations for healing.

- Begin with open discussion about the concept of the inner child - what it means, how it shows up and how the client feels about exploring this work.

- Use your choice of induction to establish comfort and guide the client into a relaxed state.

- Introduce a safe place visualisation to anchor a sense of calm and inner security. Allow time for the client to really develop this space so it feels accessible and dependable.

- If it feels appropriate, invite the inner child to appear, without pressure or expectation. It may be a visual image, a sense, a feeling, or even a knowing.

- Keep the interaction brief and observational. The focus is simply on presence and contact, not conversation. Though for some clients there will naturally be conversation.

- Guide the client to leave the child in a safe place and return with a sense of closure.

- Debrief with warmth and validation, normalising any emotional responses or resistance.

Homework: Invite the client to journal about the experience. They may also choose to draw the inner child or write a letter to them. Suggest noticing when that younger part of them shows up during the week.

Session 2:
Exploration and Emotional Awareness

Objective: Begin to explore the emotional world of the inner child and introduce supportive dialogue.

- Begin with a grounding practice or safe place induction to re-establish emotional safety.

- Use age regression or timeline work to access a memory or moment that connects to a key emotion or belief.

- Help the client identify the emotion(s) present in the memory - fear, sadness, shame, confusion, anger - and where it might still live in the body.

- Support the client in beginning a compassionate dialogue with the child part. You might offer prompts like, *"What did you need at the time that you didn't receive?"* or *"What would have made a difference?"*

- Offer the adult self a chance to validate and soothe the child's feelings, even if words are few. Presence is often enough.

- Keep the session contained. Leave the child in their safe space, and reorient the client slowly.

Homework: Encourage journalling or artwork based on the session themes. Suggest daily affirmations chosen with the child's needs in mind (e.g. *"I am enough,"* *"It's safe to feel."*).

Session 3:

Reparenting and Empowerment

Objective: Strengthen the bond between adult and child selves, and begin conscious reparenting.

- Revisit the safe place and invite the inner child to appear if it feels right.

- Encourage the adult self to check in: "*What do you need from me now?*" Let the response guide the rest of the session.

- Use visualisation or metaphor to provide nurturing. This might include wrapping the child in a blanket, sitting beside them, holding them or offering words of reassurance.

- If a memory arises spontaneously, you might use imaginary rescripting to change the emotional experience. Emphasise choice as well as safety throughout.

- Introduce an anchor, such as a hand on heart, or a comforting word or gesture, to strengthen the client's felt sense of connection to the child between sessions.

- Offer a post-hypnotic suggestion that the client can return to the feeling of care and safety whenever needed.

Homework: Encourage the client to use their anchor daily and continue connecting with their inner child through small rituals; lighting a candle, leaving a note or just taking a quiet moment to check in.

Session 4: Integration and Looking Ahead

Objective: Support the client in drawing the work together and making it sustainable in daily life.

- Open with a brief reflection on what has changed so far, however subtle.

- Use symbolic integration or parts therapy to bring the child and adult selves into closer connection, perhaps seeing them walking side by side or the child gently stepping into the adult's heart or body.

- Reinforce the client's ability to fully support themselves. You might say, *"This part of you now knows it can come to you when it needs comfort."*

- Use future pacing. Invite the client to imagine a future situation where they respond differently - with more kindness, confidence or awareness. This could be through visualisation or simple storytelling.

- Discuss ways to continue nurturing the inner child beyond therapy; self-care routines, creative expression, community, or spiritual practices.

- If the client has built enough internal safety, resilience and connection with their inner child, teach self-hypnosis for maintaining and developing the relationship.

Homework: Suggest writing a letter from the inner child to the adult self, or vice versa. Invite the client to create a visual or written "Inner Child Care Plan" as a practical reminder of what supports them.

A moment from my journey

When I first began integrating inner child work into my hypnotherapy sessions, I wanted to do everything at once. I wanted to bring the healing in fast and deep. But over time, I learned to trust the pace of the client.

One session in particular stays with me. I had planned a beautiful reparenting visualisation, but as soon as we began I sensed hesitation. Instead of pushing ahead, I paused and quietly asked if the client wanted to just sit with the child instead. She nodded.

That session became a turning point - not because of anything I said or did, but because of what I didn't do. I allowed space. I waited. And in that stillness, something happened. That was the moment I understood that it's not about the technique, it's about the relationship. Healing happens in the pauses just as much as in the process.

Notes on Adapting the Framework

- This structure is a starting point, not a strict formula. Some clients may benefit from just a few focused sessions, while others might need a longer process that unfolds slowly and gently.

- Some clients may need several sessions just to establish safety and trust, particularly if trauma, grief, or dissociation is present.

- Others may move quickly but still benefit from spending time in each phase to allow for consolidation and emotional integration.

- Trust your instincts and your client's feedback. The best progress often happens when we slow down, not when we rush through steps.

- The use of visual tools, journalling prompts, and creative exercises between sessions can greatly enhance the impact of this work.

As we begin to draw this work together, it becomes clear that healing doesn't always announce itself with big, dramatic shifts. Often, it's subtle; a softening, a moment of choice, a kinder inner voice.

A thought from me

There's no fixed map for inner child healing, only markers along the way. The real art lies in following the client's pace and knowing when to pause, deepen or wait. Sometimes progress looks like connection; other times it looks like silence or stillness.

What matters most is that we hold the space with presence and patience, allowing the client to lead the way back to themselves, step by step, at the rhythm their inner child can trust.

In the next chapter, we'll explore how to recognise and measure these quieter signs of change, so you and your clients can see and acknowledge the progress that's already unfolding.

Chapter 12
Measuring Progress and Deepening the Work

"Keep in mind that progress is not always linear. It takes constant course correcting and often a lot of zigzagging"

Buzz Aldrin

Inner child healing is often 'quiet' work, which doesn't always show itself in clear milestones or dramatic breakthroughs. More often, it reveals itself in subtle shifts; perhaps in the way a client speaks to themselves, the way they respond to stress, or the way they begin to relate to others with a little more awareness and care.

As therapists, we can become attuned to these quieter signs of healing, and we can help our clients recognise them too. Because when clients can see their own progress, they are more likely to stay engaged, more willing to keep showing up for themselves, and more able to build on the work that's already been done.

Signs of Emotional and Behavioural Progress

Progress may not always come in a straight line, but over time, there are certain signs that often emerge. You may notice when a client:

- responds to triggers with a pause or more curiosity, rather than an automatic reaction
- speaks more kindly to themselves, especially in moments of challenge
- begins to set and maintain clearer boundaries in their relationships
- feels emotions more fully without becoming overwhelmed
- takes ownership of their inner world, recognising patterns without blame
- feels more connected to their body, creativity, or intuition
- shows up with more consistency, even when the work feels difficult.

Sometimes these changes are small at first. A client might say, "I didn't beat myself up like I usually would," or "I actually said no without feeling guilty." These are powerful indicators that the younger self is being cared for and listened to. And they should be celebrated.

Progress also includes the ability to navigate setbacks with more resilience. A client who can experience discomfort or resistance and still return to the work is showing that integration is happening. They're no longer avoiding the inner child. They're learning how to stay present.

A moment from my journey

For a long time, I assumed that healing would be obvious. It would be an earth-shattering moment, a sudden flood of emotion, something big and undeniable. But that wasn't how it arrived for me. What I began to notice were small shifts, subtle changes in the way I responded to myself and the world around me.

I started catching the way I spoke to myself, and thinking about it. When things went wrong, I stopped jumping straight to blaming myself. I no longer assumed everything was my fault, or that I needed to fix everything and everyone. That in itself was a revelation.

I became more able to set boundaries. I could say no without feeling like I'd done something wrong. I stopped tying myself in knots over past relationships, stopped carrying the guilt for other people's behaviour and began to see clearly where my responsibility ended.

These shifts didn't happen overnight, and I didn't always notice them until I looked back. But they were real, and they changed everything. I realised I was treating myself with more care and kindness - not because someone told me to, but because it felt natural. I wasn't just doing the work any more. I was living it. And that was a sign, perhaps the most important one, that my inner child was no longer being ignored. She was being heard, respected, and cared for. Quite possibly for the first time.

How to Review and Reflect with Clients

Reviewing the work doesn't have to feel clinical or evaluative. It can be a warm, collaborative process that invites the client to notice their own growth. You might reflect together at the end of a session block or when it feels like a natural pause point.

Some gentle questions to invite reflection might include:

- "What feels different now compared to when we first began this journey?"
- "How do you experience your inner child today?"
- "What have you learned about yourself in this process?"
- "How do you respond to challenges now, compared to before?"

Clients are often surprised by how much has shifted when they stop to reflect. Writing or drawing about the journey can help solidify that awareness. Even looking back at early journal entries or artwork can offer a meaningful comparison.

It can also be helpful to ask, "What would your inner child say about how far you've come?" This simple question often opens the door to compassion and pride; emotions many clients rarely feel for themselves.

If appropriate, you might suggest a brief letter-writing exercise to mark the end of a phase. A letter from the adult to the child, or vice versa, can create a sense of closure and continuity.

Tools for Ongoing Deepening and Self-Support

Once a client has developed a strong connection with their inner child, the work doesn't end. It changes shape. The client becomes their own companion. They begin to hold themselves with more awareness, and with that comes an opportunity for ongoing deepening.

Some clients choose to continue working regularly, while others prefer to space out sessions, or come back when they need a reset or something else comes up. Which is fine. The goal is not dependency, but empowerment.

Encourage clients to create a toolkit for themselves. This might include:

- a daily or weekly inner child check-in; just a moment to pause, listen, and respond
- continued use of safe place visualisation or anchoring practices
- affirmations that evolve over time as their needs change
- creative expression through drawing, music, movement, or journalling
- mirror work for a few minutes each day. We all look in a mirror to brush our teeth or hair, it's an ideal opportunity to be nice to yourself
- a physical reminder of their inner child, such as a photograph, small object, or image.

You might also suggest they create an 'Inner Child Care Plan,' similar to a wellbeing plan, which outlines what helps them feel connected, grounded, and safe. This gives them a tangible resource they can return to when things feel unsettled.

Above all, remind clients that setbacks are not failures. They are part of the process. What matters is that they now have tools, awareness, and a relationship with themselves that didn't exist before.

At this stage, the focus shifts from intervention to integration. The aim is not perfection, but a more spacious way of being, where the inner child is no longer hidden, the adult self no longer burdened, and both can walk forward together with greater ease.

A thought from me

Healing often whispers before it shouts. It arrives in the pause before a reaction, in the gentler words we speak to ourselves, in the quiet courage it takes to choose differently.

These subtle moments may seem small, but they are sacred signals that something deep within is shifting. Trust those whispers. They are the roots of lasting change, unfolding softly, steadily, in their own time.

✧ ✧ ✧ ✧ ✧ ✧ ✧

In the next chapter, it's time to think about one of the most important pieces of this work – your own inner work.

Chapter 13
The Therapist's Inner Work

"In order to heal others, we first need to heal ourselves. And to heal ourselves, we need to know how to deal with ourselves"

Thich Nhat Hanh

Inner child healing is not just something we should offer to others; it's something we are continually invited into ourselves too. The work we do as hypnotherapists is relational, intuitive and innately human. It draws from our presence, our empathy and our own emotional awareness. Which means that the more attuned we are to our own inner world, the more safely and effectively we can hold space for our clients.

We don't need to go everywhere our clients go, but the more inner work we've done - and continue to do - ourselves, the more grounded and resourced we are to hold space for theirs.

Working with the inner child can touch our own unhealed places. It can stir up echoes of our past, especially when clients share experiences that feel familiar, painful or unresolved. That's not a weakness, it's an opportunity. But it does require us to be honest with ourselves, to stay resourced and to do the personal work alongside the professional.

Recognising Our Own Inner Child

Most therapists are drawn to this work for a reason. At some point, we've known what it is to feel wounded, silenced, overlooked or disconnected from ourselves. And often we've already done some work to reconnect. But inner child healing is not a box we tick, it's a relationship we build over time. And there's always 'another layer to the onion.'

Take a moment to consider your own inner child. How do they show up in your work? Do they speak through the need to get it right? Through perfectionism, people-pleasing or hesitation? Do they seek approval from clients, or fear being misunderstood? These are signs that our own child self may benefit from more care and attention.

Having compassion for our own inner reactions helps us stay grounded and humble in the therapy room. We're not striving to be perfect. We're aiming to be present.

A moment from my journey

There came a point in my practice where I realised I

couldn't just use these tools for others and leave myself behind. Not if I wanted to stay honest, present and well.

It wasn't about doing inner child work because I had to, it became something I wanted to do, something I needed to keep returning to. Not only for my younger self, but for every part of me that shows up in this work: the tired part, the hopeful part, the one that sometimes doubts, and the one that knows. It's all connected.

The more I tended to my own healing, the more spacious and intuitive my sessions became. Clients felt safer. I felt clearer.

This work doesn't just shape what I do, it shapes who I am. And I've learned that the most powerful thing I can offer as a therapist isn't technique or insight, but the steadiness that comes from doing the work myself, again and again, with patience.

The Importance of Integration and Support

It's not always easy to hold space for others who are in pain, especially when their stories mirror something in us. That's why we need spaces where *we* can be held. Whether through supervision, peer support, therapy or reflective practice, our healing matters just as much as our clients'.

Integration doesn't just happen through training or learning new techniques. It happens through slowing down, listening inward and noticing what we're carrying. Sometimes we realise we're trying to rescue a client or feeling overly responsible for their progress. Sometimes we feel flat, avoidant or emotionally drained. These are signals, not failures.

Allow yourself to be supported. This work isn't meant to be done in isolation. And the more we create space to care for ourselves, the more deeply we can care for others without becoming entangled in their process.

Practices for Self-Care and Inner Connection

Bringing self-care into your professional life isn't about ticking boxes or routines. It's about staying connected to your own needs and your own younger self. Some ways to do that might include:

- taking time after emotionally intense sessions to decompress or ground
- journalling about your emotional responses - not just completing clinical notes
- using self-hypnosis or guided recordings to reconnect with your own safe place
- checking in with your inner child at the start or end of the day
- allowing creativity, nature and movement to be part of your regulation toolkit
- recognising when rest is needed, and honouring that.

Self-compassion is a muscle. The more you use it, the stronger it becomes. And the more you live in alignment with the work you offer, the more congruent and credible your presence becomes for clients.

You may also find it valuable to revisit the tools and

techniques from this book for your own growth. Using a safe place visualisation or journalling about your younger self is not just for clients, they are resources for you too.

Holding the Mirror with Kindness

When we engage in inner child work as therapists, we're not just helping others find their way back to themselves, we're also walking our own path home. Each client we sit with becomes a mirror, a reminder, and sometimes a teacher.

It is not unprofessional to feel moved, touched or personally affected. It is human. The important thing is to have the tools, awareness, and support to process those experiences in a way that keeps both you and your clients safe.

This chapter is not here to add pressure or raise standards. It's here to offer an invitation. To honour the truth that your inner child matters too. That your wellbeing shapes the quality of the work you offer. And that healing - yours and theirs - is never separate.

A Note on Therapist Care, Burnout and Boundaries

Working closely with a client's emotional pain, especially the early wounds we touch through inner child work, can be profound and fulfilling but it can also be quietly exhausting. It's easy to underestimate the emotional load that accumulates when you consistently hold space for vulnerability, grief, shame or suppressed memories.

Even when you leave a session feeling calm or composed, your nervous system may be absorbing subtle signals. Over time, this can show up as fatigue, restlessness, over-identification with clients, or simply feeling flat and uninspired. These are not signs of failure, they're signs that something in you needs caring for.

As hypnotherapists, we often work with clients at a subconscious level. That connection can run deeper than we realise. It's vital to have ways of gently disconnecting from client material once the session ends. This might mean taking a short walk, using a symbolic closing ritual, or simply affirming to yourself, *"That belongs to them, not to me."*

Boundaries in this work aren't about shutting down. They're about staying clear, resourced, and able to show up again tomorrow. You don't need to carry your clients' pain in order to care.

Regular supervision, peer support, and space for your own healing work are essential. And so is pleasure. Creativity, laughter, movement and rest are all forms of nervous system care. They're not luxuries, but necessities for those doing deep therapeutic work.

Reflective Exercise: The Therapist Within

Take a few quiet moments, perhaps after a session or at the end of your day. You might like to place a hand on your heart or simply sit with your breath before beginning.

Let the following questions guide your reflection. You may choose to journal your responses, speak them aloud, or simply notice what arises:

- *When I think about my own inner child, what do I see? What do I feel?*
- *How does this part of me show up in my work with clients?*
- *What helps me stay grounded, clear, and present?*
- *What signals let me know I need support or nourishment?*
- *How can I care for myself, not just as a therapist but as a whole person?*

If you like, end with a gentle affirmation or reminder, something your own inner child might need to hear today.

- *I'm doing the best I can, and that is enough.*
- *I hold space for others and still honour myself.*
- *I am allowed to rest, reset, and be supported too.*

Self-Hypnosis for Ongoing Support

Self-hypnosis can be a valuable part of long-term care, both for therapists and stabilised clients. It offers a way to stay connected to the inner child, manage emotional waves between sessions, and reinforce feelings of safety and self-trust.

This doesn't need to be complicated. It might involve returning to a favourite safe place in the mind, revisiting a nurturing message from a previous session, or simply pausing to tune in to what the inner child needs that day.

Clients can be encouraged to practise moments of self-hypnosis at home, using affirmations, breathwork, or guided recordings to help them reconnect and regulate. For therapists, it becomes a space to restore, reflect, and remain grounded in your own healing journey; a reminder that inner child work isn't just something we do for others, but something we continue to honour in ourselves.

You might even create a simple self-hypnosis script for clients to use, or guide them to develop their own phrases and images that bring calm and connection.

A thought from me

You can't pour from an empty cup. Take care of yourself first. Each time you pause to listen inward, check in with your own child self, or give yourself permission to rest, you're topping up that cup. And when you do, you have so much more to give - not just as a therapist, but as a whole, feeling human being.

This is your work and it is also your path. Let it evolve. Let it support you. Let it be real and human and enough. Because you are enough, just as you are. In the next chapter, we bring it all together.

Chapter 14
Bringing It All Together

"The past has no power over us. It doesn't matter how long we have had a negative pattern. The point of power is in the present moment. What a wonderful thing to realize! We can begin to be free in this moment!"

Louise Hay

As hypnotherapists, we have the privilege of holding space for deep and meaningful healing. Inner child work is not about fixing anyone; it's about helping them reconnect with the parts of themselves that were lost, silenced or pushed aside. It's about rebuilding trust, restoring a sense of safety, and nurturing self-love and acceptance from within.

A moment from my journey

I remember the first time I truly felt those words, that the past no longer had to define me, that I could choose something different in the present moment. I'd read them in books, heard them in workshops, seen them on affirmation cards, but I don't think they'd really landed. Not deep down. Not in the place where old wounds still shaped how I saw myself.

It wasn't a spectacular, all lights blazing, breakthrough. It came one morning, during a quiet visualisation. I'd been revisiting an old memory, one I'd spent years trying to make sense of, when something changed. The familiar shame didn't rise. The need to explain or justify didn't appear. Just a calm voice inside saying, "That's not who you are now."

That moment didn't erase the past. It didn't need to. What it did was loosen its grip. It reminded me that I wasn't stuck in those old stories anymore. That I could breathe, choose, move forward, not in defiance of the past but in freedom from it.

Since then, I've had many reminders. Some subtle, some stirring. But that one moment gave me a deeper knowing: healing isn't about forgetting what happened. It's about reclaiming who we really are beyond what happened. That's what I hold for myself. That's what I hold for my clients.

Throughout this book, we've explored:

- the foundations of inner child theory
- techniques and approaches to support healing through hypnosis

- structures for multi-session work and long-term integration
- the emotional presence and steadiness required to guide clients safely through this process.

But more than that, I hope this journey has reminded you of the quiet power of being present. Of truly witnessing. Of listening without judgement, and creating space for younger parts of the client's self to be seen – the ones that may have never been seen or heard – to come forward, often for the first time, and to be met with care and compassion.

When we work with the inner child, we:

- invite clients to feel without fear
- empower them to reparent and then support themselves
- encourage lasting shifts in identity, self-worth and emotional wellbeing.

You won't always see instant change. But you'll often feel it – perhaps a flicker of trust, a moment of connection. These are signs that healing is beginning. And it matters more than you might realise.

As you reach the end of this this book, I encourage you to reflect:

- How has your understanding of the inner child changed or deepened?
- What have you learned about your own healing, or capacity to hold space for someone else's?

- Which tools or approaches feel most aligned with your unique style as a therapist?

Continue learning. Continue listening. And most of all, continue showing up with commitment, care and quiet courage.

Because when you help someone heal their inner child, you don't just change one life, you help shift generations.

I hope what you've found here supports and inspires your practice. Thank you for doing this work. Thank you for being part of this journey.

Jackie Thomson

Reclaiming the Lost Parts

*We don't go back to erase the past,
but to gather what was left behind -
the parts still waiting
to be seen,
to be safe,
to be loved.*

*Healing begins quietly:
a kinder thought,
a new choice,
a moment of presence.*

*We don't push the inner child forward.
We sit beside them.
We stay.
We show them
I'm here now.
You're not alone.*

*And slowly trust returns.
Not because we changed what was,
but because we changed what we believe
about ourselves.*

*In choosing to return,
again and again,
we find our way home.*

Resources & Further Reading

Books

Homecoming: Reclaiming and Championing Your Inner Child - John Bradshaw

Healing the Shame that Binds You - John Bradshaw

You Can Heal Your Life - Louise L. Hay

When the Body Says No - Dr. Gabor Maté

Healing the Child Within: Discovery and Recovery for Adult Children of Dysfunctional Families – Dr. Charles L. Whitfield

Parts Therapy: A Client-Centered Approach for Hypnotherapists - Roy Hunter

No Bad Parts: Healing Trauma and Restoring Wholeness with the Internal Family Systems Model - Dr. Richard Schwartz

Loving What Is -loving what is by Byron Katie

The Dram of Being a Child: The Search for the True Self – Alice Miller

Therapy, Training & Tools

www.jackiethomson.com for therapy, training and online resources

Inner Child Healing & Hypnosis: The Companion Guide - download at: www.jackiethomson.com/icguide

About the Author

Jackie Thomson is an advanced clinical hypnotherapist, trainer and coach based in North Wales, who aims to help people live happier, healthier lives.

Working predominantly with midlife women, Jackie often blends hypnotherapy, Heal Your Life® coaching, intuitive insight and other holistic skills, along with an extensive experience and understanding of the inner child. Her unique approach supports clients in overcoming challenges, often rediscovering their true selves along the way. She also offers training for hypnotherapists with a focus on ethical, heart-led practice, and is always happy to guide others in weaving inner child work into their client sessions in a way that feels safe and effective.

Before stepping into the world of healing and hypnotherapy, Jackie ran her own successful corporate business for nearly 30 years, until a personal turning point set her on a new path. That path led to Louise Hay's *Heal Your Life®* training, to spiritual growth, to learning, unlearning, and ultimately to helping others heal.

As a published author, speaker and a clear voice for community, wellbeing, self-compassion and the power of change, she was named one of the UK's SmallBiz100 in 2024, and has won several awards for hypnotherapy.

2025 sees her speaking at the UK Hypnosis Convention for the third consecutive year, and receiving the Prestige Holistic Therapist of the Year award for Wales.

When she's not working, you'll often find her walking on the beach, crocheting, supporting her elderly mum, or perhaps planning her next wellbeing event or community initiative.

You can find out more about her work and download free resources at www.jackiethomson.com.

Index

Abandonment: 18, 25, 26
Adapted Child: 17
Adapting the framework: 91
Affirmations: 57, 73, 88, 99, 109, 110
Affirmations (the power of): 59
Affirmations (the power of): 59
Age regression: 69
Anchor: 45, 46, 69, 80, 86, 89, 99
Archetypes: 15, 25, 29
Assessing emotional readiness: 34
Awareness: 9, 46, 87
Body awareness: 46
Boundaries: 47, 107
Breath focus: 46
Burnout: 107
Carl Jung: 15
Child Archetype: 15
Child Ego State: 16
Clean language: 44, 69
Comfort: 4, 26, 72, 86, 90
Consent: 9, 38
Core Archetypes: 25
Compassion: 7
Creative expression: 10, 81, 90, 99
Defectiveness: 18
Divine child: 27
Ego state: 16, 78
Emotional deprivation: 18

Emotional safety: 30, 34, 41, 43, 47, 55, 85, 87
Empowerment: 80, 88, 99
Eternal child: 27
Ethical awareness: 9
Fear: 13, 16, 17, 19, 20, 26, 27, 43, 53, 71 78, 88, 115
Forgiveness: 61, 82
Forgiveness (the power of): 61
Future Pacing: 90, 108
Gestalt Therapy: 19
Grounding techniques: 45
Growth beyond the session: 63
Guilt: 63
Imaginary rescripting: 79, 89
Informed consent: 9
Inner bonding: 19
Inner child: 1, 7, 13, 25, 33, 41, 57, 67, 78, 86, 87, 89, 90, 95, 103, 113
Innocent Child: 26
Integration: 72, 77, 79, 80, 82, 85, 90, 96, 100, 105
Internal Family Systems: 20
Journal/journalling: 73, 82, 87, 88, 92, 99, 106, 109
Kindness: 10, 29, 58, 62, 73, 90, 107
Little Professor: 17
Loneliness: 3, 26
Louise Hay: 57, 62
Magical child: 26
Mapping archetypes to wounds: 29
Meeting the inner child: 70
Metaphor: 45, 54, 73, 89
Mirror: 61, 63, 99, 107

Mirror work (the power of): 61

Moments from my journey: 3, 8, 14, 28, 37, 42, 52, 58, 68, 80, 91, 97, 104, 110

My thoughts: 5, 11, 22, 31, 39, 49, 55, 64, 74, 82, 92, 100, 104, 110

Natural Child: 17

Nature child: 26

Needy child: 27

Neglect: 26

Non-judgemental presence: 48

Orphaned child: 26

Parts/ego state therapy: 78

Parts Therapy: 19, 78, 90

Perfectionism: 2, 104

Power of language: 43

Presence: 8, 42, 48, 70, 86, 88, 103, 106, 115

Recognising our own inner child: 104

Recognising resistance: 51

Reconnection: 64, 77

Reflect and review with clients: 98

Reflective exercise: the therapist within: 108

Regression: 9, 21, 69, 87

Rejection: 20, 25, 53, 79

Reparenting: 64, 72, 88, 115

Rescripting: 79, 89

Resilience: 9, 34, 36, 80, 90, 96

Resistance: 51, 53, 54, 61, 82, 87, 96

Responsibility: 61, 63

Sadness: 2, 48, 88

Safe place: 45, 46, 54, 69, 86, 89, 99, 106, 109

Safe place visualization: 46, 69
Safety: 20, 27, 30, 34, 36, 39, 41, 47, 69, 72, 80, 85, 86, 89, 90, 92, 109, 113
Safety before strategy: 41
Schema Therapy: 17
Script: 7, 15, 100
Self-care and inner connection: 106
Self-Hypnosis: 73, 90, 106, 109, 110
Self-hypnosis for ongoing support: 109
Sensory grounding: 46
Session 1: Connection and safety: 86
Session 2: Exploration and Emotional Awareness: 87
Session 3: Reparenting and empowerment: 88
Session 4: Integration and looking ahead: 90
Shame: 18, 25, 27, 53, 63, 88, 107
Signs a client may not be ready (yet): 36
Signs of emotional and behavioural progress: 96
Somatic: 78, 96
Somatic memory retrieval: 78
Stability and support: 35
Strategies for navigating resistance: 54
Subconscious: 13, 19, 21, 33, 41, 43, 45, 51, 53, 60, 62, 67, 69, 73, 80, 108
Subjugation: 18
Supervision: 10, 105, 108
Therapist care: 107
Timeline: 80, 87
Transactional Analysis: 16
Trauma: 2, 4, 7, 9, 26, 35, 46, 74, 78, 92
Trauma sensitivity: 9

Triggers: 10, 21, 96
Understanding resistance as protection: 53
Unmet needs: 1, 8, 25, 67
Validation: 2, 15, 21, 27, 71, 87
Visualisation: 21, 46, 52, 58, 63, 69, 72, 74, 80, 86, 89, 90, 99, 107
Voice Dialogue: 20
Vulnerability: 2, 17, 53, 55, 107
Why resistance arises: 53
Witnessing: 7, 69, 115
Wounded Child: 26
Younger self: 28, 36, 44, 61, 63, 70, 74, 79, 96, 106

Printed in Dunstable, United Kingdom

66250110R00087